Praise for *The Shortest History of Democracy*

'The best, most readable book on the radical potential of democracy' **Professor Takashi Inoguchi, Tokyo University**

'Remarkable... It covers a vast historical landscape while also delivering intellectual depth.'
Professor Matthew Flinders, University of Sheffield

'Shortest – and best! Provocative, passionate, fun, and even a bit hopeful' **Professor Michael Schudson, Columbia University**

'A short, concentrated but deep analysis. Those who do not know will learn... those who know will also learn.'
Professor Xavier Philippe, University of Sorbonne

'[Keane is] the pre-eminent scholar of the history of democratic ideas... A gem of a book.' **Professor Paul 't Hart, Utrecht Univ.**

'An insightful history of democracy, a perceptive reflection on its fragility and an intelligent and original analysis of its present problems.' **Enrique Krauze, author of *Redeemers: Ideas and Power in Latin America***

'Engaging, accurate, witty, well-referenced, short and well-structured' **Pedro Aibéo, Architectural Democracy**

'Free of the rhetoric that many in the West use to justify their flawed systems, honest about the complexities of living democratically, and uncompromising in intellectual an... clarity.' **Professor Cherian George, Hong Ko...**

'For cynics and idealists alike, thi... better time.' **Scott Ludlam, ...**

'An urgent, important book fo...
Professor Glyn Davis, Department ... ...inister and Cabinet, Canberra

THE SHORTEST HISTORY OF DEMOCRACY

JOHN KEANE

PICADOR INDIA

Also by John Keane (selected works)

To Kill a Democracy: India's Passage to Despotism (with Debasish Roy Chowdhury; 2021)

The New Despotism (2020)

Power and Humility: The Future of Monitory Democracy (2018)

When Trees Fall, Monkeys Scatter: Rethinking Democracy in China (2017)

Democracy and Media Decadence (2013)

The Life and Death of Democracy (2009)

Global Civil Society? (2003)

Václav Havel: A Political Tragedy in Six Acts (2001)

Reflections on Violence (1996)

Democracy and Civil Society (1988)

Also in the Shortest History series

The Shortest History of China by Linda Jaivin

The Shortest History of India by John Zubrzycki

The Shortest History of the Soviet Union by Sheila Fitzpatrick

The Shortest History of the World by David Baker

In memory of C.B. Macpherson (1911–1987), wise teacher, modest master of words, democrat

First published in Great Britain 2022 by Old Street Publishing Ltd
First published in India 2023 by Picador India
an imprint of Pan Macmillan Publishing India Private Limited
707 Kailash Building
26 K. G. Marg, New Delhi 110001
www.panmacmillan.co.in

Pan Macmillan, The Smithson, 6 Briset St, Farringdon, London EC1M 5NR
Associated companies throughout the world
www.panmacmillan.com

ISBN 978-93-90742-86-8

5 7 9 8 6 4

Text design and typesetting by Marilyn de Castro

Printed and bound in India by Thomson Press India Ltd.

FSC www.fsc.org MIX Paper | Supporting responsible forestry FSC® C010615

Contents

AGE OF ASSEMBLY DEMOCRACY	2500 BCE	First popular assemblies in Syria-Mesopotamia
	1500 BCE	Republics governed by assemblies spring up on the Indian subcontinent
	1450 BCE	Linear B script of the Mycenaeans includes words such as *dāmos* and *dāmokoi* 
	1100 BCE	Phoenician popular assemblies develop
	650–600 BCE	Greek assemblies begin to flourish
	507 BCE	Transition to democracy begins in Athens 
	460–370 BCE	Life of Democritus, the laughing democrat
	336 BCE	Dēmokratia, the goddess of democracy, appears in an Athenian law sculpted in marble
	260 BCE	Macedonian troops finally crush the Athenian democracy
AGE OF ELECTORAL DEMOCRACY	600s CE	Birth of Islam and the custom of *wakil* (representing legal, commercial and religious matters on behalf of others)
	930	Faroe Islands and Icelandic assemblies
	1188	First parliaments born in northern Spain 
	1215	The signing of the Magna Carta (a great charter of freedoms)
	1414–1418	Council of Constance, where the bishops elect a Pope
	1600	The Divine Covenants Resistance to tyranny in Scotland
	1644	John Milton's *Areopagitica* Defence of liberty of the press
	1649	Public execution of King Charles I Brief period of republican government in England
	1765	Marquis d'Argenson defines 'true' democracy in representative form
	1776	US Declaration of Independence Birth of a self-governing republic
	1789	French Revolution Execution of Louis XVI

	1791	Thomas Paine's best-selling *Rights of Man* 
	1820s	Birth of multi-party competition in elections Rise of caudillos in Spanish America
	1835–40	Alexis de Tocqueville's classic *Democracy in America* published in two volumes
	1835–40	Introduction of the secret ballot
	1890s	Voting rights for women in New Zealand, South Australia, Colorado, Utah and Idaho, and parts of Canada 
	1900	Early welfare state reforms in Uruguay
	1920–1939	Destruction of electoral democracy by purple tyranny, military dictatorship and totalitarianism World War II begins
AGE OF MONITORY DEMOCRACY	1945	Formation of the United Nations Reinhold Niebuhr's *The Children of Light and The Children of Darkness*
	1948	Adoption of Universal Declaration of Human Rights
	1950s	New Indian constitution (26 January 1950) and first general election (October 1951 – February 1952)
	1960s	Civil rights networks, sit-ins and teach-ins Rebirth of feminism, gay rights, disability rights and other social movements
	1972	First green political parties formed in Australia and New Zealand
	1974	Carnation revolution in Portugal 
	1989	Velvet revolutions in Central-Eastern Europe Collapse of the Soviet Union
	1990s	Nelson Mandela freed (11 February 1990) and end of apartheid (27 April 1994) Celebrations of the global triumph of liberal democracy 
	2000s	Populist backlashes in Brazil, Italy, Poland, Mexico and other countries Expanding global power of new despotic regimes in China, Russia, Turkey and Saudi Arabia
	2020	Coronavirus pandemic Sweden's V-Dem Institute reports marked global decline of support for democracy

MILLIONS OF CITIZENS AROUND THE WORLD are today asking questions of grave importance: what's happening to democracy, a way of governing and living that until recently was said to have enjoyed a global victory? Why is it everywhere reckoned to be in retreat, or facing extinction? They're surely right to wonder.

Three decades ago, democracy seemed blessed. People power mattered. Public resistance to arbitrary rule changed the world. Military dictatorships collapsed. Apartheid was toppled. There were velvet revolutions, followed by tulip, rose and orange revolutions. Political rats were arrested or put on trial, suffered death in custody or were shot on the spot.

Now things are different. In Belarus, Bolivia, Myanmar, Hong Kong and other places, citizens are the victims of arrest, imprisonment, beating and execution. Elsewhere, democrats generally seem to be on the back foot, gripped by feelings that our times are weirdly unhinged, and troubled by worries that big-league democracies such as India, the United States, Britain, South Africa and Brazil are sliding towards a precipice, dragged down by worsening social inequality, citizen disaffection and the rot of unresponsive and corrupted governing institutions. Fears are growing that democracy is being sabotaged by angry popular support for demagogues, or by surveillance capitalism, pestilence, the rise of China, ruinous wars, and Putin-style despots who speak the language of democracy but don't care a fig for its substance. At the same time, complacency and scepticism are on the rise: there are those who say talk of the sickness and coming death of democracy is mostly melodrama – overheated description of what is only a passing period of political reckoning and structural readjustment.

The Shortest History of Democracy is inspired by these tough questions and doubts to offer a compact reply: while practically all democracies are facing their deepest crisis since the 1930s, we are by no means in a replay of that dark period. Yes, powerful economic and geopolitical forces are once again gaining the upper hand against the spirit and substance of democracy. The great pestilence that began sweeping the world in 2020 has made things far worse, as an influenza pandemic did a century earlier. The old adage that ordinary folk count for nothing and democracy is a cloak for the rich is surely still partly true. So is the spread of whip-hand policing and surveillance of disillusioned citizens. With the gradual decline of the United States, the re-emergence of a self-confident Chinese empire and the unending disorders and savagery occasioned by the break-up of the Soviet Union and Arab-region despotism, our times are hardly less tumultuous or momentous. And yet – the qualification is fundamental – our times are so troubling and puzzling exactly because they *are* different.

A HOPEFUL HISTORY

Understanding how our times are unique requires us to take the past seriously. But why? How is the remembrance of things past not just helpful but vital in considering the fate of democracy in these troubled years of the twenty-first century? Most obviously, history matters because when we are ignorant of the past we invariably misunderstand the present. We lose the measure of things. Unforgetting makes us wiser. It helps us make better sense of the new trials and troubles faced by most present-day democracies.

There's something else. This slim book sets out to stir up a sense of wonder about democracy. It's no antiquarian encounter with things past, a history for the sake of history. It's more like an odyssey filled with unexpected twists and turns, a story of those defining moments when democracy was born, or matured, or came to a sticky end. The book tracks the long continuities, gradual changes, crises and sudden upheavals that have defined its history. It pays attention to past shocks and setbacks when democracy suffered a crushing blow, or committed democide. It puts its fingers on puzzles – why democracy has typically been portrayed as a woman, for example – and springs a few surprises. It also aims to unsettle orthodoxies.

History can make mischief. This book bids farewell to the cliché that democracy was born in Athens and the bigoted belief that the early Islamic world contributed nothing to the spirit and institutions of democracy. It makes the case for a world history of democracy and therefore rejects political scientist Samuel P. Huntington's influential but one-eyed claim that the most important development of our generation is the 'third wave' of American-style liberal democracy triggered by events in southern Europe in the early 1970s. It shows why democracy is much more than periodic 'free and fair' elections, as Huntington thought, and why the birth of a new form called monitory democracy in the years after 1945 has been far more consequential, and remains so today.

There is one thing this book is not: a gloomy tale of catastrophes. In paying attention to democracy's braided fortunes, it does not strengthen the spirits of doubters and despots by warning in know-it-all fashion that, when it comes to democracy, everything usually ends badly. The book agrees with the distinguished French classics scholar Nicole Loraux: the history of democracy has principally been recorded by its enemies, such as the ancient Greek historian and military general Thucydides (c. 460–400 BCE) and the Florentine diplomat and political writer Niccolò Machiavelli (1469–1527). By contrast, these pages take the side of democracy, but they try hard to ditch illusions and biases and guard against the danger that history can come to resemble a big bag of tricks played by the living on the dead. Democracy has no need of memory police. This short book doesn't suppose that it is the last word on democracy because it knows everything about its past; or that it knows in advance that, despite everything, all will turn out well, or badly. It's neither foolishly optimistic nor dogmatically pessimistic about the future. It is, rather, the bearer of hope.

The spiky defence of democracy running through these pages draws strength from the remembrance of the fallen.

In the build-up to the November 2020 US election, Asian-American artist Amanda Phingbodhipakkiya (1992–) partnered with the civil society advocacy group MoveOn to produce posters designed to counter disinformation and inspire disillusioned citizens to cast their votes and 'continue fighting for their right to do so'.

It is inspired by encounters with a host of oft-forgotten characters who ate, drank, laughed, sighed, cried and died for democracy, people from distant pasts whose inspiring words and deeds remind us that democracy, carefully understood, remains the most potent weapon yet invented by humans for preventing the malicious abuse of power. The book investigates the obscure origins and contemporary relevance of old institutions and ideals, such as government by public assembly; votes for women, workers and freed slaves; the secret ballot; trial by jury; and parliamentary representation. Those curious about political parties, periodic elections, referenda, independent judiciaries, truth commissions, civil society and civil liberties such as press freedom will get their fill. So too will those interested in probing the changing, often hotly disputed meanings of democracy, or the cacophony of conflicting reasons given for why it is a good thing, or a bad thing, or why one impressive feature of democracy is that it gives people a chance to do stupid things and then change their minds, and other jokes useable at any election-night party.

Among the funniest jokes about democracy, said Hitler's Reich Minister of Propaganda Joseph Goebbels, is that it gives its enemies the means to destroy it – and, we could add, grind its memories into the dust of time. Let's take this fascist bad joke to heart. Several times in the past, democracies have stumbled, and fallen, and sometimes never recovered. This book is a precautionary tale, but it has a sharp edge. It shows that history isn't storytelling that sides with the enemies of democracy. It is not an epitaph, a sad tale of ruin recorded in prose and footnotes. To paraphrase the eighteenth-century sage Voltaire (1694–1778), it is not the sound of silk slippers upstairs and wooden clogs below. Far from being a sequence of horrors, it shows that history can come to the defence of underdogs. History is not obituary; it can inspire by reminding us that the precious invention called democracy is usually built with great difficulty, but so easily destroyed by its enemies, or by thoughtlessness, or by lazy inaction.

AGAINST TITANISM

Although democracy has no built-in guarantees of survival, it has regularly been the midwife of political and social change.

Here we come to a puzzling point with far-reaching consequences. Democrats not only altered the course of history – for instance, by shaming and dumping monarchs, tyrants, corrupt states and whole empires run by cruel or foolish emperors. It can be said – here's a paradox – that democracy, understood simply as people governing themselves, helped make history possible. Its birth implied something that continues to have a radical bite: that humans could invent institutions that allow them to decide, as equals, how they will live together on our planet. This may seem rather obvious, but think about its significance for a moment. The idea that breathing, blinking mortals could organise themselves into forums where they deliberate on matters of money, family, law and war as peers and decide on a course of action – democracy in this sense was a spine-tingling invention because it was in effect the first-ever *malleable* form of government.

Compared with political regimes such as tyranny and monarchy, whose legitimacy and durability depend upon fixed and frozen rules, democracy is exceptional in requiring people to see that everything is built on the shifting sands of time and place, and so, in order not to give themselves over to monarchs, emperors and despots, they need to live openly and flexibly. Democracy is the friend of contingency. With the help of measures such as freedom of public assembly, anti-corruption agencies and periodic elections, it promotes indeterminacy. It heightens people's awareness that how matters are now is not necessarily how they will be in future. Democracy spreads doubts about talk of the 'essence' of things, inflexible habits and supposedly immutable arrangements.

It encourages people to see that their worlds can be changed. Sometimes it sparks revolution.

Democracy has a *sauvage* (wild) quality, as the French thinker Claude Lefort (1924–2010) liked to say. It tears up certainties, transgresses boundaries and isn't easily tamed. It asks people to see through talk of gods, divine rulers and even human nature, to abandon all claims to an innate privilege based on the 'natural' superiority of brain or blood, skin colour, caste, class, religious faith, age or sexual preference. Democracy denatures power.

By encouraging people to see that their lives are open to alteration, democracy heightens awareness of what is arguably the paramount political problem: how to prevent rule by the few, the rich or the powerful, who act as if they are mighty immortals born to rule? Democracy solves this old problem of titanism – rule by pretended giants – by standing up for a political order which ensures that the question of who gets how much, when and how is kept permanently open. From its inception, democracy recognised that if humans were not angels, they were at least good enough to prevent others from behaving as if they were. And the flipside: since people are not saintly, nobody can be trusted to rule over others without checks on their power. Democracy supposes, the Chinese writer Lin Yutang (1895–1976) once said, that humans are more like potential crooks than honest gentlefolk, and that since they cannot be expected always to be good, ways must be found of making it impossible for them to be bad.[1] The democratic ideal is government of the humble, by the humble, for the humble. It means rule by people, whose sovereign power to decide things is not to be given over to imaginary gods, the stentorian voices of tradition, autocrats or experts, or simply forfeited to unthinking laziness, allowing others to decide matters of public importance.

Chinese satirist and writer Lin Yutang at work on his invention, a Chinese-character typewriter. His writings mocked the propaganda and censorship of the 1930s Nationalist government. The first of his many English-language books, *My Country and My People* (1935), became a bestseller.

SURPRISES AND SECRETS

Since democracy encourages people to see that nothing of the human world – not even so-called human nature – is timeless, its history is punctuated with extraordinary moments when, against formidable odds, and despite all expectations and predictions, brave individuals, groups and organisations defied the status quo, toppled their masters and turned the world upside-down. Democracy often takes reality by surprise. It stands on the side of earthly miracles. The dramatic arrest and public execution of kings and tyrants, unplanned mutiny of disgruntled citizens, unexpected resistance to military rule and cliffhanger parliamentary votes are among the dramas that catch the living by surprise and leave those who come after fascinated by how and why such breakthroughs occurred.

Making sense of these dramas of democratic triumph is challenging. It requires letting go of ground-solid certainties. It forces us to open our eyes in full wonder to events made more marvellous by the fact that democracy carefully guards some of her oldest and most precious secrets from the prying minds of later generations.

Consider an example: the fact that democracy in both ancient and modern times has often been portrayed as a woman. The 2019 protests that led to the overthrow of the Sudanese dictator Omar al-Bashir included a white-robed student protester, Alaa Salah, who was revered for her spirited crowd-dancing and calls for demonstrators to stand up for dignity and decency. The 2019 summer uprising of Hong Kong citizens against mainland Chinese rule saw her appear, thanks to crowdsourced funding, as a four-metre-high statue, equipped with helmet, goggles and gas mask, clutching a pole and an umbrella. In the ill-fated 1989 occupation of Beijing's Tiananmen Square, democracy, designed by students from the Central Academy of Fine Arts, appeared as a goddess bearing a lighted lamp of liberty.

Going back in time, the Italian artist Cesare Ripa of Perugia (c 1555–1622) depicted democracy as a peasant woman

Alaa Salah, symbol of a people's uprising, atop a car and dressed in a white thoub, leading chants for the overthrow of President Omar al-Bashir in Khartoum in April 2019.

holding a pomegranate – a symbol of the unity of the people – and a handful of writhing snakes. And, thanks to the work of twentieth-century archaeologists, we have evidence of a goddess named Dēmokratia worshipped by the citizens of Athens (who were all male) in exercising their right to resist tyranny and to gather in their own assembly, under their own laws.

Our detailed knowledge of her in that context is limited; in matters of democracy, time's arrow doesn't fly in a predictably clear line. But we do know that the noun used by Athenians for nearly two centuries to describe their way of life – *dēmokratia* – was feminine. We also know that democratic Athens had the firm backing of a deity – a goddess who refused marriage and maternity, and was blessed with the power of moulding men's hopes and fears. Athenians did more than imagine their polity in feminine terms: democracy itself was likened to a woman with divine qualities. Dēmokratia was honoured and feared, a transcendent figure blessed with the power to give or take life from her earthly supplicants – the men of Athens. That was why a fleet of Athenian warships was named after her, and why buildings and public places were adorned with her image.

In the 1643 French edition of Cesare Ripa's *Iconologia* (1593), a widely read book of emblems and virtues, democracy is presented as a coarsely dressed peasant woman. Until well into modern times, democracy was dismissed as a dangerously outdated (Greek) ideal that licensed the uncouth and the unwashed.

In the north-west corner of the public square known as the agora, nestled beneath a hill topped by a large temple that survives today, stood an impressive colonnaded building, a civic temple known as the Stoa of Zeus Eleutherios. The interior was lavishly decorated, with a glorious painting of Democracy and the People by a Corinth artist named Euphranor. Exactly how he portrayed them remains a riddle. The paintings have not survived, yet they serve as a reminder of the intimate link between democracy and the sacred, and of the vital role of the belief in Athens that a goddess protected its polity.

The point is driven home by the most famous surviving image of Dēmokratia from ancient Athens. Carved in stone above a law from 336 BCE, it shows the goddess adorning, shielding and sheltering an elderly bearded man who represents the *dēmos*, the people. There's evidence that the goddess Dēmokratia attracted a cult following of worshippers, and that her sanctuary was also located in the agora. If that's true, there would have been a stone altar on which citizens, assisted by a priestess, recited prayers of gratitude and offered sacrifices, such as cakes, wine and honey, a slaughtered goat or a spring lamb. There might have been *theoxenia*, invitations to the imagined goddess to dine as guest of honour while reclining on a splendid couch.

The priestess, duty-bound to ensure the goddess was shown due respect, would have been appointed from a leading Athenian family, or nominated or chosen by lot, perhaps after an oracle was consulted. A female operator in a man's world, the priestess had mysterious authority that could not be profaned, except at the risk of punishment, which ranged from cold-shouldering and bad-mouthing to exile and death. In return, the priestess helped to protect democratic Athens from misfortune.

The arrangement had a corollary. The misbehaviour of the public assembly – for example, foolish decisions by its prominent citizens – risked payback, such as the failure of the olive crops, the disappearance of fish from the sea or, as we are going to see, democide: the self-destruction of democracy.

PART ONE

Assembly Democracy

THE OPENING EPISODE OF THE HISTORY of democracy saw the birth of public assemblies – gatherings in which citizens freely debated, agreed and disagreed, and decided matters for themselves, as equals, without interference from tribal chiefs, monarchs or tyrants. Let's call it the age of assembly democracy.

The origins of this age come shrouded in uncertainty. Some have tried to spin the story that the roots of democracy are traceable to Athens. Ancient Greece, they say, is where it all began.

The idea that democracy was made in Athens stretches back to the nineteenth century, courtesy of figures such as George Grote (1794–1871), the English banker-scholar-politician and co-founder of University College London. It tells how, once upon a time, in the tiny Mediterranean town, a new way of governing was invented. Calling it *dēmokratia*, by which they meant self-government, or rule (*kratos*) by the people (*dēmos*), the citizens of Athens celebrated it in songs and seasonal feasts, in stage dramas and battle victories, in monthly assemblies and processions of proud citizens sporting garlands of flowers. So passionate were they about this democracy, runs the story, that they defended it with all their might, especially when spears and swords rimmed their throats. Genius and guts earned Athens its reputation as the wellspring of democracy, as responsible for giving democracy wings, enabling it to deliver its gifts to posterity.

FROM EAST TO WEST

The Athens legend still grips the popular imagination and is repeated by scholars, journalists, politicians and pundits. But here's the thing: it's false.

Let's begin with the word itself. 'Democracy' has no known wordsmith, but in the mid-fifth century BCE, the word *dēmos* appeared in Athenian inscriptions and in literary prose; perhaps it was used earlier, but few inscriptions survive before this period, and prose written between c. 460 and 430 BCE has been lost. Antiphon (c. 480–411 BCE), one of the pioneers of public oratory, mentions in his 'On the Choreutes' the local custom of making offerings to the goddess Dēmokratia. The historian Herodotus (c. 484–425 BCE) speaks of her. So does the military commander and Athenian political pamphleteer Xenophon (c. 430–354 BCE), who dislikes the way democracy weakens oligarchs and aristocrats. There's also an important passage on democracy in *The Suppliants*, a tragedy by Aeschylus. First performed around 463 BCE and a great favourite of Athenian audiences, it reports a public meeting at which 'the air bristled with hands, right hands held high, a full vote, democracy turning decision into law'.

So far, so simple. But there's evidence that the d-word is much older than commentators on classical Athens have made out. We now know that its roots are minimally traceable to the Linear B script of the Mycenaeans, seven to ten centuries earlier. This late Bronze Age civilisation centred on the fortified city of Mycenae, located to the south-west of Athens, in today's orange- and olive-growing region of Argolis. For more than 300 years, its military held sway in much of southern Greece, Crete, the Cyclades islands and parts of south-west Anatolia in western Asia. It is unclear exactly how and when the Mycenaeans began to use the two-syllable word *dāmos* (or *dāmo* 𐀅𐀗) to refer to a group of powerless people who once held land in common, or three-syllable words such as *dāmokoi*, meaning an official who acts on behalf of the *dāmos*. But it's possible that these words, and the family of terms we use today when speaking about democracy, have origins further east – for instance, in the ancient Sumerian references to the *dumu*, the children of a geographic place who share family ties and common interests.

Archaeologists have made another discovery that contradicts the Athens legend. The first models of assembly-based democracy sprang up in the lands that correspond geographically to contemporary Syria, Iraq and Iran. The custom of popular self-government was later transported eastwards, towards the Indian subcontinent where, from around 1500 BCE, assembly-based republics first appeared. As we'll see, assemblies also travelled westwards, first to Phoenician cities such as Byblos and Sidon, then to Athens, where during the fifth century BCE it was said with swagger to be unique to the West, a sign of its superiority over the politically depraved 'barbarism' of the East.

Evidence suggests that this period began around 2500 BCE, in the geographic area that's today commonly known as the Middle East. There, public assemblies formed in the vast river basins etched from desert hills and mountains by the Tigris and Euphrates rivers and their tributaries, and in the cities that sprang up for the first time in human history.

The ancient Syrian-Mesopotamian cities of Larsa, Mari, Nabada, Nippur, Tuttul, Ur, Babylon and Uruk today mostly resemble windswept heaps of grey-brown earth. But around 3200 BCE, they were centres of culture and commerce. Their imposing temples, the famous *ziqqurats* – often built on massive stone terraces or gigantic artificial mountains of sundried bricks – made travellers gasp with delight. Typically situated

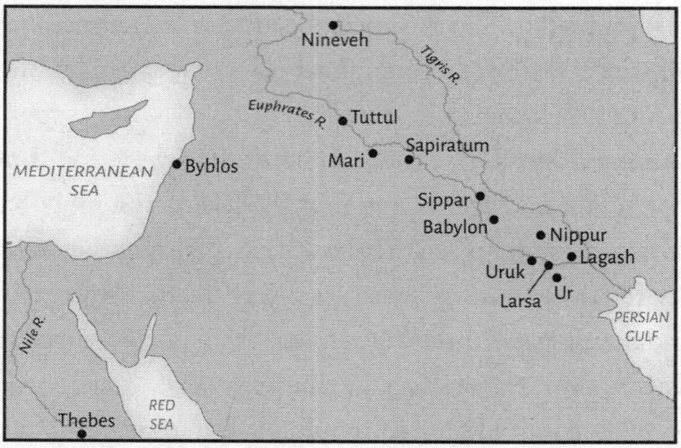

Established in areas of fertile soil and abundant water, the principal ancient cities of Syria-Mesopotamia were the cradles of self-government by assemblies between c. 3200 and 1000 BCE.

at the centre of an irrigated zone, where land was valuable, these places reaped the bounty of dramatic local increases in agricultural production. They fostered the growth of specialised artisan and administrative skills, including scribes' use of the rectangular-ended stylus to produce wedge-shaped cuneiform writing, and they served as conduits of long-distance trade in such raw materials as copper and silver.

The cities varied in size from 40 to around 400 hectares; they felt crowded in a way our earth had never before known. Their dynamics shaped every feature of Syria-Mesopotamia, including its patterns of government. Kings are conventionally thought to have dominated this region during these centuries. But permanent conflicts and tensions – over who got how much, when and where – shaped the institution of kingship on matters such as land ownership and trade. In fact, kings of the time were not absolute monarchs – despite what later historians with Western prejudices have said. Archaeological evidence confirms that, at least 2000 years before the Athenian experiment with democracy, the power and authority of kings was restrained by popular pressure from below, through networks of institutions called 'assemblies'. In the vernacular, they were known as *ukkin* in Sumerian and *pŭhrum* in Akkadian.

For this insight that assemblies functioned as a counterweight to kingly power, we're indebted to the Danish scholar Thorkild Jacobsen (1904–1993). He identified what he termed a flourishing 'primitive democracy' throughout Syria-Mesopotamia, especially in early second millennium Babylonia and Assyria. He liked to say that, to its peoples, the region resembled a political commonwealth owned and governed by gods, who were widely believed to gather in assemblies – with the help of humans, who formed assemblies in imitation.

Was there any substance in Jacobsen's idea of 'primitive democracy'? There are doubts. The teleology lurking within the word 'primitive' – the inference that this was the first of its kind, a prototype for what was to follow – raises tricky questions about the historical connections between the assemblies of the Greek and Mesopotamian worlds. It also supposes that despite the many differences in the character and practice of democracy across time and space, there is an unbroken evolutionary chain that links assembly-based democracy and modern electoral democracy, as if the vastly different peoples of Lagash and Mari and Babylon were brothers and sisters of James Madison, Winston Churchill, Jawaharlal Nehru, Margaret Thatcher and Jacinda Ardern. There's the risk of overstretching the word 'democracy' as well. If terms such as 'primitive democracy' (or 'proto-democracy', coined around the same time by the Polish-American anthropologist Bronisław Malinowski) are used too freely, we fall into the trap of characterising too many societies as 'democratic' just because they lack centralised institutions and accumulated monopolies of power, or because they prohibit violent oppression. Matters aren't helped by the anachronistic use of the word with Linear B origins, 'democracy'. And then there is the least obvious but most consequential objection: by calling the assemblies of Syria-Mesopotamian 'primitive', there is a danger of overlooking their *originality*.

But Jacobsen's work remains important because it reminds us that the ancient assemblies of Syria-Mesopotamia are the fossils present in the ruins of Athens and other Greek democracies, and the assemblies of the later Phoenician world. These much older assemblies of Syria-Mesopotamia teach us to rethink the origins of democracy. They invite us to see that democracy of the Greek kind had Eastern roots, and that today's democracies are indebted to the first experiments in self-government by peoples who have been, for much of history, written off as incapable of democracy in any sense. *Ex oriente lux*: the lamp of assembly-based democracy was first lit in the East, not the West.

Thorkild Jacobsen in Iraq, taking notes during the clearance of a large residential quarter in the ruins of the Sumerian city Tell Asmar, c. 1931–1932.

IMITATING THE GODS

What did these assemblies look like? How did they function? Here we come across something both fascinating and puzzling. These early citizens' assemblies were inspired by myths that gave meaning and energy to people's everyday lives.

For the people of Syria-Mesopotamia – as for Greeks 2000 years later – the cosmos was a conflict-ridden universe manipulated by powerful forces with individual personalities. These deities had emerged from the watery chaos of primaeval time, and they were to be feared because they controlled everything: mountains, valleys, stones, stars, plants, animals, humans. Their fickleness ensured that the land was racked periodically by thunderstorms, which caused torrential rains and halted travel by turning the ground to mud. The local rivers rose unpredictably at their command, smashing barriers and inundating crops. Scorching winds smothered towns in suffocating dust at the deities' behest.

The whole world was in motion, yet it was said that the deities had won an important victory over the powers of chaos and had worked hard to bring energy and movement into the world, to create order through dynamic integration. The resulting balance was the outcome of negotiations that took place in an assembly – a divine council that issued commands to decide the great coming events, otherwise known as destiny.

There were reckoned to be some fifty gods and goddesses, but the shots were called by an inner circle of seven. The most influential figure was Anu, the god of the sky, a rider of storms who convened the 'ordained assembly of the great gods'. These gods were believed to have the ability to grant some of their powers to humans. Their favour could be bought. In Syria-Mesopotamia, getting a god was a means of self-empowerment. Letters were written to the gods, and festivals of wailing processions calling on them to act aroused popular interest. In every dwelling there was a shrine to the household's chosen god, who was worshipped and presented with daily offerings. The practice of mimicking the gods' self-governing methods was supposed to have the same effect: by emulating their capacity for oratory and collective decision-making, normally through negotiation and compromise based on public discussion, the earthly arts of self-government could flourish. So in Syria-Mesopotamia, the custom of gathering together to decide things had pagan and polytheistic roots. When citizens of various occupations and standing gathered to consider some or other matter, they thought of themselves as participating in the world of the deities, as suppliants of their benevolence.

Anu, also called An in Sumerian, was considered the divine personification of the sky, the ancestor of all ancient Mesopotamian deities and demons, and the supreme source of authority for the other gods and all earthly rulers. In at least one text, he is described as the figure 'who contains the entire universe'.

Deep Christian and modern prejudice against this kind of mythical thinking later ensured that the ancient assemblies of Syria-Mesopotamia went unrecognised in histories of democracy. Something else played a part in this ignorance: the political economy of literacy. Writing was first used to facilitate the ever more complicated accounting that had become vital for the expanding cities and temple economies. The surviving evidence suggests that while writing enabled the birth of a significant literature in Syria-Mesopotamia, literacy was limited to elites. Recordkeeping was mostly for tracking trade and commerce, and for the administration of public institutions, such as temples and palaces, and so restricted to governmental institutions and the wealthy. This had the effect of rendering the assemblies mostly invisible to later observers. The effect was reinforced, paradoxically, by the strength of these assemblies: exactly because centralised bureaucracies such as the palace monopolised economic and administrative recordkeeping, the decentralised politics that took place in the assemblies went unrecorded – or so the evidence implies.

The old Sumerian and Akkadian words for assembly, *ukkin* and *pŭhrum*, are believed to refer, as in English, to both an informal gathering of people and a governing body. Some of them were rural. During the second millennium, for instance, tent-dwelling pastoralists from north-west Mesopotamia gathered regularly to thrash out matters of common concern. City meetings to hear disputes and issue legal judgements were commonplace. The assemblies' mandate included the power to tread on the toes of monarchs – as noted in a political text called *Advice to a Prince*, a clay tablet recovered from

Advice to a Prince was copied from the original text around 700–650 BCE and stored in the Library of Ashurbanipal, a collection of approximately 30,000 stone texts uncovered in the 1840s in the ancient Assyrian city of Nineveh.

the world's oldest library, at Nineveh, in modern-day northern Iraq. Written in Babylon towards the end of the second millennium BCE, it warned monarchs that the gods and goddesses would not look kindly upon their meddling with the freedoms of city and country life. If a greedy prince 'takes silver of the citizens of Babylon and adds it to his own coffers' or 'hears a lawsuit involving men of Babylon but treats it frivolously', Marduk, lord of heaven and earth, 'will set his foes upon him [and] will give his property and wealth to his enemy'. Similar penalties were listed for such wrongdoings as the failure to heed advice, the improper conviction or unjust imprisonment of citizens, and attempts to force citizens to work in the fields or temples. The text reminded princes, present and future, that the assemblies of Babylon, Nippur and Sippar had each established – with divine help – immunity from despotic or arbitrary rule: 'Anu, Enlil, and Ea, the great gods who dwell in heaven and earth, in their assembly affirmed the freedom of those people from such obligations.'[1]

Sceptics might understandably ask: for the powerful, weren't assemblies mighty useful political tools – an ear to the ground for princes otherwise deafened by distance from their subjects? And didn't assemblies also operate as channels for mobilising support in favour of princely policies – so giving these a more-than-fighting-chance of being adopted?

Assemblies were indeed vital channels of communication between governors and governed in small communities, where rulers found it virtually impossible to avoid mixing with those over whom they exercised power. But like the Greek democracies that followed more than a millennium later, the ancient assemblies of Syria-Mesopotamia were venues in which public learning, as well as the suspicion of power and the art of what would later be called politics (making judgements in public about who gets how much, when and how), were cultivated. In the country and the city, these assemblies shaped people's lives. They played a role in matters ranging from disputes over water and land to questions of taxation and public safety. Over time, popular assemblies were based within the larger temples of cities. These temples, especially during the first millennium BCE, served not only as places of worship but also as spaces of deliberation and buffers against arbitrary exercises of governmental power. That was true too of the local assemblies within a city: each quarter had its residents' assembly, which doubled as a court of law that heard and resolved disputes among neighbours.

The polycentric quality of the ancient assemblies of Syria-Mesopotamia ensured that they were not just organs of local monarchs, or of the temples, or of rich and powerful imperial rulers. They were a formidable political force in their own right. But how inclusive were they? We know that attendance at some assemblies was genuinely large. The assemblies weren't secular – the distinction between the sacred and the profane wasn't meaningful to the peoples of the region, as it wasn't for the Greeks. The elders of a city typically played a guiding role. While the evidence either way is thin, it seems doubtful that women were regularly included. Slaves and children normally had no voice. But there is a record of a domestic slave attending an assembly meeting in the merchant city of Kanesh. From the Old Babylonian period (c. 1700 BCE) there's also a record of an assembly attended by all residents – the men and women of every background and occupation – of an outpost on the Euphrates called Haradum, whose mayor, Habasanu, was accused of embezzling taxpayers' funds.[2] Elsewhere, potters, gardeners, bird-catchers and soldiers in service of the local temple were among the 'commoners' who sat regularly in assemblies. There were gatherings convened by particular crafts or professions, such as merchants. There is even some interesting evidence, from exactly the same time as Athenian democracy was blossoming, suggesting the existence of self-governing associations of foreigners, like the assemblies of Egyptian and other immigrants in fifth-century Babylonia. Such assemblies never happened in Athens.

BYBLOS AND A PAPYRUS SCROLL

These early assemblies proved geographically contagious. They spread eastward, into what is today the Indian subcontinent, where sometime after 1500 BCE, in the early Vedic period – a thousand years before Athenian democracy – republics governed by assemblies became common.[3] Thanks to the river trade and caravan routes that filtered through Syrian-Mesopotamian cities such as Mari and Tuttul and Nabada, the custom of assembly-based deliberations migrated westwards, towards the Mediterranean coasts that came to be controlled by the Phoenician sea peoples, as well as towards our Greek cousins, who cheekily claimed for themselves the honour of inventing assemblies by giving them a new name: democracy.

A rare papyrus scroll discovered in the late nineteenth century, miraculously preserved in the desert sands of Egypt, reveals the important role the Phoenicians played in keeping assemblies alive. It documents the misfortunes of a diplomat named Wen-Amon, from the city of Thebes. He travelled by sea around 1100 BCE to the thriving Phoenician port of Byblos, 700 kilometres east of Athens. There, his envoy was to purchase from local merchants fine-quality timber hewn from the cedar forests of the nearby mountains. The business was straightforward: with the permission of the local prince, the cedar would be loaded onto a ship by slaves, freighted to the east end of the Mediterranean Sea, unloaded in Thebes and transformed by the best local craftsmen into a river barge, to be used in the sacred fleet of Egyptian ruler Ramesses XI (c. 1100–1070 BCE), in honour of Amon, the god of fertility and patron of pharaohs.

Despite protracted wrangles about payment, and delays caused by winter snow, the timber was eventually hauled by a team of 300 oxen and loaded onto the ship anchored at the Byblos port. But hours before setting sail, the fickle deities struck. Poor Wen-Amon and his crew found themselves surrounded by a hostile fleet of eleven ships manned by the neighbouring Theker people. Upset by his trade, they demanded his arrest by the local authorities. A large crowd, puffing with excitement, gathered around the crescent-shaped harbour. A message was sped by runner to the local prince, Zakar-Ba'al, calling upon him to resolve the crisis. Confusion reigned. Wen-Amon and his crew feared for their lives.

The prince arrived at the harbour. To calm tempers, he provided the envoy with flagons of wine, a sheep for roasting and a songstress to spread cheer. The prince informed Wen-Amon that he wanted to take measure of the dispute and consider his options overnight. 'When morning came,' reads the rare document, Zakar-Ba'al 'had his *mw-'dwt* summoned, and he stood in their midst, and he said to the Theker: "Why have ye come?"'[4]

The document records that Wen-Amon and his men were escorted safely beyond the harbour, where strong winds filled their sails, giving them a porpoise start on the Theker pirates. The rest of what happened at Byblos remains unclear, which doesn't much matter here because the details are uninteresting compared to the strange little word – *mw-'dwt* – that appears in the text. Some archaeologists either leave this masculine noun in transcript form – 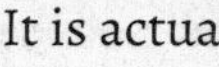 – or they translate it, misleadingly, as 'bodyguard'. It is actually an old Semitic word for 'assembly' or 'council' (*mô'ēd* in Hebrew), and it is used in Biblical passages, such as the reference to those who are 'famous in the congregation', the 'men of renown' who gather in 'the assembly' (Numbers 16:2). The same word crops up in Exodus 27:21, where Moses commands the Israelites to fetch oil made from hand-crushed olives: 'Aaron and his sons shall arrange for [the lamps to burn], from evening until morning, in God's presence, in the assembly tent.'

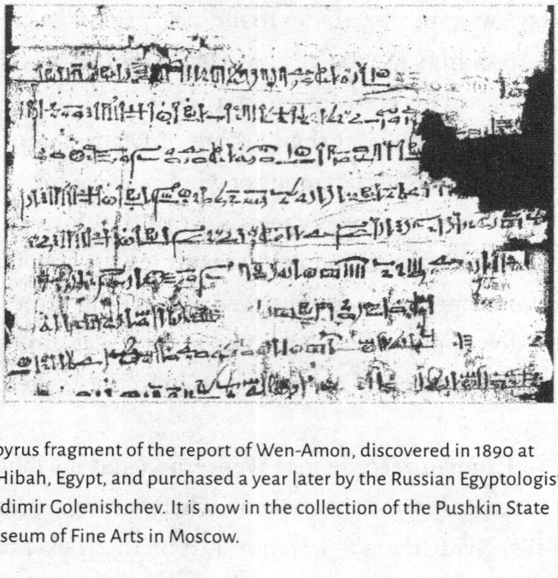

Papyrus fragment of the report of Wen-Amon, discovered in 1890 at al-Hibah, Egypt, and purchased a year later by the Russian Egyptologist Vladimir Golenishchev. It is now in the collection of the Pushkin State Museum of Fine Arts in Moscow.

EARLY GREEK ASSEMBLIES

Wen-Amon's tale tells us that a species of self-government existed a full five centuries before the Athenian experiment with democracy. At the time of his expedition, Byblos – later called Gebal and today known as Jbeil, located in the troubled republic of Lebanon – was a small but thriving maritime city-state. Its reputation ran high in the ancient world of the Mediterranean not only for its wood and paper – some treasured words such as 'book' (*biblìon* = booklet), 'Bible' (*biblos* = papyrus, scroll) and 'bibliography' are associated with it – but also for its system of government by assembly. It even gets a mention in the Bible, where the region is described as a zone of free trade and commerce. 'Thy borders are in the midst of the seas,' runs a well-known passage, which tells not only of the prized wheat, honey, oil and balm from the land of Israel and fine-quality ship masts hewed from the ancient cedars of Lebanon, but also speaks of an assembly comprising 'the elders of Gebal and her wise men' (Ezekiel 27:9).

The story of Wen-Amon bears a more general point: thanks to the Phoenicians, democratic assemblies took root among the Greek-speaking citizen states scattered throughout the Mediterranean. These assemblies initially flourished quite separately from Athens – certainly well before the last decade of the sixth century BCE, when the citizens of that city began to build a democracy. Evidence of these early assemblies has been ravaged by time. The fragments that survive have not been blessed with the intense efforts at archaeological resuscitation applied to Athens. Matters have been made worse by the sloppy organisation of underfunded museums, and by the private pilfering of the treasures in their collections. Yet traces of reliable evidence still remain – such as the reference to 'the *dēmos*' on a reddish volcanic rock, found in southern Chios and dated to 575–550 BCE, and a small block of grey schist from the temple of Apollo Delphinius at Dreros, dated to 650–600 BCE. This chunk of stone is of great interest because it may be the oldest surviving Greek law, and the first to mention 'the *damioi*', a body involved in deciding matters of common concern to the city.

The Dreros law carved on this stone reads: 'The city has thus decided; when a man has been a *kosmos*, the same man shall not be a *kosmos* again for ten years. If he does act as a *kosmos*, whatever judgements he gives, he shall owe double, and he shall lose his rights to office, as long as he lives, and whatever he does as *kosmos* shall be nothing. The swearers shall be the *kosmos* and the *damioi* and the twenty of the city.'

We now know that there were altogether some 200 Greek citizen states such as Dreros and Chios. Up to half of them tasted democracy at one time or another. The details of these early *dēmokratiai*, as they were locally known, aren't altogether good news for today's democrats. They suffered defeat and destruction, either by military conquest, or by conspiracies of the rich, or by single-minded tyrants; or by all three forces, in some combination or sequence. Their bad fortune reminds us of the utter contingency of democracy – of just how easily it can be scattered to the winds.

But there were plenty that endured, some of them predating Athens by more than a generation. These resilient assemblies teach us to consider the wide variety of ways in which democracy can be built and can survive difficulties. They also alert us to the amazing diversity of species of assembly democracy.

Consider the prosperous island state of Chios, located just five miles off the coast of Asia, where, around 575–550 BCE, a maritime democracy was founded. The polity depended on a sizeable slave-labour population engaged in viticulture and an elite exporting that wine and trading in commodities. Rich landowners wielded considerable political clout, and it's probable they tried to enforce their will on a council of magistrates, a body that the islanders called the *boule demosie* – which is why a stone tablet on public display reminded the aristocracy daily to behave themselves, to remember that the final say in public matters belonged to the *dēmos*.

Among the oldest and most fascinating cases of Greek democracy is the Corinthian-founded citizen state of Ambracia. The colony was established sometime between 650 and 625 BCE, on the bend of a navigable river a few miles inland

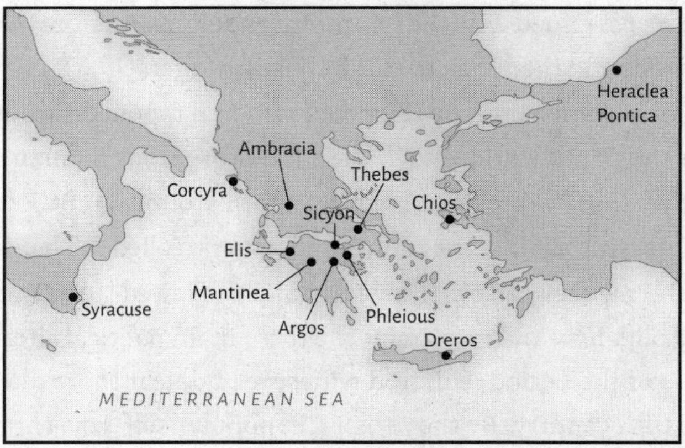

Ancient Greek democracies dating from the seventh century BCE included citizen states on both the mainland and the islands of the Mediterranean.

from the sea, in the midst of a fertile wooded plain. Self-government by public assembly there dates to around 580 BCE – more than seventy years before the assembly in Athens was convened. True to the rule that democratic states are rarely founded democratically, the assembly-based democracy of Ambracia was born of an uprising against the harsh rule of dictator Periander. He apparently aroused widespread indignation after rumours circulated that, during a heavy drinking session, he had asked his young male lover whether he had yet fallen pregnant. The slight caused by that remark in a society tolerant of male homosexuality yet ambivalent towards women is barely understandable to us. So grave was the insult that it seems to have caused Periander's spurned lover to hatch a plot to overthrow the ruler. He galvanised a coalition of the local *dēmos* and Periander's enemies – presumably disaffected property holders. According to Aristotle, 'the *dēmos* joined with the tyrant Periander's enemies to throw him out and then took over the constitution itself'.[5]

Government run by the poorest men happened throughout the Greek world – such as in the prosperous Sicilian city of Syracuse, where democracy was born around 491 BCE with an uprising against the ruling landowners (called the *hoi gamoroi*). Practically all other towns in Sicily followed suit; tyranny and oligarchy and monarchy, the three main political alternatives of the period, suffered widespread defeat there during the fifth century. By the 460s BCE, popular self-government had also come to a number of cities in southern Italy, to the sickle-shaped Ionian island of Corcyra (today's Corfu) and to the Peloponnesian mainland. From one of its states, Elis, comes an intriguing inscription, the tail end of a lengthy law dating probably from the early years of the fifth century BCE. It shows that in Elis, written laws could be superseded not by a court judgement (*dika*), but only by means of a public enactment that had the consent of a body called the 'whole people assembled' (*damos plethyon*).

For some time, neighbouring Mantinea had also been a vibrant farming democracy governed by a class of small landholders called the *dēmos ho georgikos* – a social group that was the backbone of the best and oldest kind of democracy, in Aristotle's opinion. In Mantinea, as in maybe 100 other citizen states of the Greek world, assembly democracy proved to be a novel cure for tyranny and the abuse of power – a new method of self-government that was practised throughout the region, including most famously in Athens, where, during the course of the fifth century BCE, democracy came to mean rule by an assembly of adult male citizens.

THE RISE OF ATHENIAN DEMOCRACY

What was life like in Athens, once considered the birthplace of assembly democracy? Around 507 BCE, when the transition to democracy began, its resident population numbered about 30,000 men, slaves, women and children. As democracy took root, that figure doubled. It was swelled by tens of thousands of foreign residents, called *metics*, and by traders and travellers who entered its gates annually, passing through its winding, crooked streets and into the arms of a city that locals thought had been blessed by the deities.

The Pnyx, a bowl-shaped open-air amphitheatre on a hill overlooking the city, was where their assembly met. Athenian citizens also had another public space: the agora, located beneath the north-west slope of the Acropolis. This town square was considered the hub of their city-state, which became the most powerful in the Greek world. And they thought of themselves, proudly, as a democracy. By that, the democrats of Athens meant that their polity was owned collectively: not just by men from prominent families or wealth, but also by carpenters, farmers, shipbuilders, sailors, shoemakers, spice sellers and blacksmiths. Democracy was valued as a form of government in which the people ruled as equals, citizens banding together and rescuing themselves, collectively and individually, from the natural ruin brought on by the passing of time and the progression towards death. By countering human frailty, places such as the agora and the Pnyx functioned as public shelters. They provided a sense of what Athenians called *aidós*: meaningful well-being and mutual respect. It was as if these public spaces infused citizens with a sense of grounded reality, daily confirmed by the presence of others. That is what the melancholic 'weeping philosopher' Heraclitus (c. 540–480 BCE) meant when he said that the awake shared a common public world, whereas those who took no interest in the city's affairs were in effect asleep, turning their backs on the polity to pursue private interests.

Athenian democracy wasn't secular in any recognisably modern European sense. Current-day champions of 'deliberative democracy' and citizens' assemblies often claim that

The Acropolis at Athens (1846), an idealised image of democratic Athens at its height, portrays affluent and well-educated citizens gathered in the agora, below the Parthenon and the Acropolis (which is topped by the colossal statue of Athena).

their proposals are true to the founding spirit of Athenian-style democracy, but this is to forget that the entire ethos of assembly democracy blended the sacred and the profane, to the point where talk of the separation of religion and politics would have made no sense to Athenians. Its democracy had room for dissenters, certainly. In the early 440s BCE, the first sophist, Protagoras of Abdera (481–411 BCE), told Athenians that man was the measure of all things – including the deities, who perhaps existed only in men's minds. Others probably agreed, or pondered the same thought in silence. But the reality was that Athenian democracy was widely seen through supernatural eyes. Athenians learned from an early age, through religious cults and the rituals practised within their households, that life was anchored in a polytheistic universe of gods and goddesses – and that this community of deities infused the earthly democracy with a strong sense of sacred standards.

As in Syria-Mesopotamia, the citizens of Athens invested great hopes in their deities. They also feared them. The public trial and execution of the philosopher Socrates in 399 BCE for importing false gods into the city, and for impiously corrupting its youth, confirmed that individuals who snubbed the acknowledged deities would suffer harsh punishment. The priests and elders loved to remind citizens of a story taken originally from Homer: that at the entrance of the home of Zeus, the god of freedom, stood two large barrels; from these he dispensed ill to some newcomers, good to others, and to the rest a few ladles of good from one barrel and a bit of ill from the other. Such tales put the whole city on edge.

We may scoff at these deep feelings for the sacred. But many citizens of Athens truly believed that gods such as Zeus would punish the polity – for instance, by bringing foul weather or failed harvests, or the death of oak trees – if its members behaved unjustly.

The Athenians' fear of gods and goddesses had a flipside, for they believed that the deities put a spring in the step of mortals. The deities gave guidance, offered protection and imbued the lives of the devout with meaning. Put more exactly: they helped Athenians cope with the contingencies of life. Not only did their presence explain natural disasters and otherwise inexplicable events, such as droughts and epidemics;

they could come to the rescue, especially in sticky situations, when wise solutions to problems had to be found. They also helped define the vital issues. Divination – approaching gods and goddesses, or consulting the female oracles, whose job was to pass on messages from the deities – reminded citizens of their mortality, and of their need for humility. The deities daily alerted Athenians to the need to practise the delicate art of peaceably approaching those who might prove capricious or dangerous, negotiating with them and reaching decisions made on the basis of mutual trust and respect. Divination also served as a brake on leaders who were too clever by half, or too headstrong to consider others. It put power on a leash.

There was a striking resemblance between the methods of divination and democracy. There were many Athenian gods and goddesses, but no clear revelations, no sacred books, no official creeds. The deities were partisan – they conspired and took sides – but they were open to persuasion; there was room for playing noughts and crosses with them. So just as the deities had to be approached, consulted and their advice interpreted before decisions could be made, so democracy was a practice in which citizens felt moved to gather respectfully in public, to decide as equals how they should live together, in the face of broader uncertainty. The relationship between the deities and humans was unequal; the gods and goddesses had the power to inconvenience or to destroy human beings. But it was exactly that power imbalance that made it necessary for citizens in the agora to please the deities by mimicking their customs.

GENDER, SLAVERY AND POWER

The worship of the goddess Dēmokratia was part of this equation. Athenian democracy was a deeply gendered affair. Democracy was protected by a goddess, but many male citizens still supposed a sharp division between the public life of the agora and the privacy of the household – where women became pregnant and suffered the tearing pains of childbirth, their children were raised on stories and myths and taught to read and write, and cleaning, food preparation and other daily chores were done with the help of domestic servants. The good citizen came equipped with a phallus, which reminds us too that there were deep connections between homosexuality and democracy in its Athenian form. Its democracy was a phallocracy. Waited on by underlings, men bonded and ruled as equals. They formed associations and spent much time together in public. They drew pleasure from their efforts to preen young boys for public life. Men mingled, held hands and kissed in the company of others. The display of male affection and love was tied to the intensive pursuit of physical beauty, the lust after pleasure and the deep aversion to growing old – at the expense of women and slaves.

The whole system of Athenian democracy rested upon slavery. That fact later tormented democrats, as we are going to see. But in Athens the connections ran so deep and wide that an outside observer might have been forgiven for thinking that democracy was a clever alibi for the enslavement of the many by the few. The same observer might have seen that within Athenian democracy some citizens grew wealthier,

The goddess Dēmokratia crowning the personified Dēmos – the people – in an Athenian relief dated to around 336 BCE.

giving them the means to import and acquire slaves, especially for work in agriculture, manufacturing and mining. That was why the growth of democracy went hand in hand with the expansion of slavery, and why owning slaves was a much-prized benefit of citizenship.

Slavery of course predated democracy, and there were many types of slaves, but to be a citizen meant being a cut above a slave, who was merely a human being (*anthropos*). There were no political parties or trade unions in democratic Athens. Slaves were the property of citizens. They could be bought and sold, bequeathed or confiscated, penetrated or beaten, according to the whims of their masters. In the richer households, slave women worked as maids, cooks, bakers, seamstresses, knitters and hairdressers; male slaves were servers, housekeepers, doorkeepers and attendants for the male children. Meanwhile, entertainers, dancers and prostitutes, male and female, serviced the carnal needs of citizens, whether in cheap brothels or in the luxurious ambience of drink-soaked symposia.

Slave labour was used extensively in marble quarrying, while in the lead- and silver-mining industries, ruthless exploitation generated great wealth for the polity and produced individual fortunes (a leading fifth-century military general, Nicias, reportedly owned 1000 slaves, whom he hired out as miners, under the supervision of a trusty Thracian slave named Sosias). Slaves were heavily involved in specialist crafts, such as lyre-making and tannery, as well as in the manufacture of goods such as clothing, weapons, knives, lamps and pots and pans. They helped build and repair roads. They worked in the government mint, cleaned streets and even served as bouncers who kept order in the assembly, in the courts and in the agora. Their sweat was invested in temple repairs and public building programs, for instance on the Acropolis and at the sanctuary of Eleusis, located a day's walk west of Athens.

Given Athens' reliance on slave labour, it's significant that very few extended poems, plays or philosophical texts of the period defended slavery. It may be that the most oft-quoted example, from Aristotle, was not at all representative of the range of views held by Athenian citizens. Many slave owners seemed to suffer an ailment that could be called democratic anguish, either because they felt pangs of shame or because they knew from practical experience that when they treated their slaves as beasts they never got the best from them. A famous Athenian law against hubris displayed the ambivalence. Carried over from pre-democratic times, it was designed to protect poorer citizens against being treated like slaves. The law specifically outlawed acts of gratuitous violence bent on their humiliation and abuse. Yet it went further, stipulating that anyone who killed a slave was required to undergo a purification ceremony to appease the deities – and could expect to face legal action, perhaps even the charge of homicide, initiated by another master. Orators frequently spoke in defence of the law, heaping praise on the 'generosity' of Athenians and sometimes pointing out that the law implied the banning of *all* types of hubris against *all* residents of Athens.

PARRHĒSIA AT THE PNYX

In an age before the printing press, mass media and internet, when news and rumours were circulated by the wheel, the horse or word of mouth, oratory was an Athenian specialty. Athens was a literate polity, in the sense that at least some of its citizens could read aloud to others if necessary. But the oratory it became known for was on display at the Pnyx, where the whole citizen body, called the *ekklesia*, met to decide laws that governed the city-state. Sessions there were often blustery. 'The city is full of freedom and unrestrained speech and there is licence within it for a man to do as he likes,' complained an enemy of democracy, the philosopher Plato (c. 427–347 BCE), who went on to note that the echoes produced by the rock walls of the Pnyx 'redouble the din of the criticism and the praise'.[6]

The speakers' platform at the Pnyx, within sight of the Acropolis, is where sometimes lengthy orations were delivered to the assembly.

Plato's complaint seems overdone. There's much lingering evidence of citizens' self-discipline. They were acutely aware of the dangers of violent feuds (they called them *stasis*), and there's no doubt that within the assembly, threatened or actual violence was not tolerated. Well-trained heralds plus detachments of archers and slaves were usually on hand to enforce its rules and customs. Citizens, seated in the round on bare rock, propped up on their elbows or lying on cushions brought from home, expected others to respect the obligation to speak spontaneously, to trade in what they called frank speech, or *parrhēsia*. There were jokes aimed at the rich and charges of disreputable private behaviour. There was talk of corruption and signs of disquietude about the type of blind arrogance called *hybris*. Sessions were sprinkled with satire: speakers commonly persuaded others by making them laugh. There were hijinks and moments of self-mockery. Some sessions resembled the closing scene of a much-loved satire by Aristophanes (445–385 BCE), *Knights*, in which the figure of old man Demos is jabbed and jostled by a slave and a sausage seller.[7]

But the assembly was often gripped by sobriety. Speakers issued reminders that to be a citizen meant being the 'equal and peer' of others. It was often said that democracy was a special type of government that enabled each citizen to enjoy *isonomia* (equality before the law), the entitlement to speak and the freedom to 'rule and be ruled in turn'. The spirit of democracy was summarised by the skilled orator and pre-Socratic philosopher Democritus (c. 460–370 BCE). The well-run polity, he liked to say, is the strongest protection against human greed and folly; if the polity is safe, all is safe, whereas if it is lost, all is lost. Democracy is the best form of polity because it ensures frank speech. It gives a hard time to the foolish and to the arrogant. Frank speech fosters the spirit of equality and mutual aid; it counters selfish desires and ambitions with cheerfulness (*euthymia*). According to Democritus, democracy, by protecting frank speech, also ensures that the mistakes of men who held office are remembered longer than their successes.

DIRECT DEMOCRACY?

The celebration of frank speech in the Athenian assembly was combined with hostility to factions and suspicion of political factions in particular. There was no great love of majority rule; the preference was for consensus decision-making. Even voting (*diaphora*) was regarded with some suspicion because it meant disagreement and division in the polity. Civil war was a constant fear. Athens was a no-party democracy that dreamed of reaching unanimous decisions through public debate that produced unquestionably good decisions.

This belief in the binding power of public assembly later came to be seen as the greatest advantage of 'direct' or 'pure' democracy. Today's friends of deliberative democracy, those who say its quintessence is cool-headed public deliberation by citizens, hearken back to Athenian democracy as a form of government not only of the people and for the people, but also by the people – to a far greater extent, and much more meaningfully, than in today's large states and non-governmental organisations. Such thinking is traceable to the eighteenth-century Genevan political thinker Jean-Jacques Rousseau (1712–1778). 'Among the Greeks,' he claimed, 'all that the people

David Van Reybrouck, author of *Against Elections* (2016) and champion of deliberative democracy, observing a meeting of Belgium's first country-wide citizen assembly, the G1000 Citizens' Summit, held on 11 November 2011.

had to do, they did themselves. They met constantly in public assembly. They lived in a mild climate. They were not greedy. Slaves did all the necessary work. The people's main concern was with their own liberty.'[8]

Never mind the slavery, the subordination of women or the belief in the deities, and the fact that Athens wasn't the birthplace of assembly democracy. The fans of direct democracy typically overlook the point that 'the people' cannot in practice govern unless chosen representatives are empowered to handle certain tasks on its behalf. Exactly because all citizens cannot be in the same place at the same time to handle a range of different matters, democracy requires deputation. The specialisation of tasks shows that 'the people' can never act as an undivided body. Such a group may try to imagine itself standing shoulder to shoulder, listening ear to ear. But self-government requires delegates, whose decisions on behalf of the group invariably trigger political tensions among citizens.

The assembly democracy of Athens illustrates these unavoidable dynamics of representation. We'll look at them in more detail in the coming pages, but for now it's enough to say that for all the praise of its exemplary qualities as a 'direct' or 'participatory' democracy, several kinds of mediating institutions stood in the way of the fiction that Athens was a system based on the direct rule of the sovereign *dēmos*. One was the powerful body known to Athenians as the Areopagus, the seat of the oldest and most august court in Athens, a kind of fifth-century House of Lords.

Then consider the way that in the name of the *dēmos*, Athenians performed duties vicariously for others. Every citizen was eligible for a year's service to a body known as the Council of Five Hundred. Its citizen-senators certainly weren't parliamentary representatives in our modern sense: required to swear an oath to serve the *dēmos* faithfully, they had no direct power to make or amend laws. Rather, they resembled a steering group or a supervisory executive, whose main job was to draft and guide legislation for the assembly. The other functions of the council changed over time but included such essential tasks as the inspection of ships and cavalry, and the scutiny of newly allotted officials to determine their fitness for office in a process known as *dokimasia*. It tried magistrates accused of wrongdoing and worked with public bodies responsible for matters such as the leasing of mines and the sale of confiscated property.

The Council also elected by lot, again on a rotating basis, a small inner group of fifty senators known as *prytaneis*. Aged thirty or over, these senators were paid to supervise the day-to-day administration of the government, as well as to handle disputes among citizens. They were expected to serve for one-tenth of the year (one *prytany*) and sometimes to work overnight. While Athens slept, these paid senators kept watch over the city.

In these and other ways, the citizens of Athens, in the name of the people, placed their interests in the hands of others. The odd thing is that the word 'representation' and its more modern meanings were unknown to Athenians. Only in the nineteenth century did Greeks come to have a word – *antiprosopos* – for speaking directly about 'representation', which initially had the rather strange meaning of standing before or opposite someone or something, for instance an enemy or opponent on the battlefield. The Athenian assembly sometimes spoke of an 'appointed messenger', such as an envoy or ambassador, whose job was to convey decisions or requests to a foreign power. They also had a word for 'guardian' or 'steward', who was entrusted with supervising arrangements already agreed by citizens. Yet 'representation' was not in their political dictionary.

A random selection machine known as a *kleroterion*, used to choose jurors to serve within Athens' various courts of law.

The question of language is important, because it was as if Athenians could not say with accuracy what they were doing. They also had no lexicon for understanding what would later be called the separation of powers, even though the demarcation and disbursement of political offices was commonplace. Athens had no civil service or bureaucracy in today's sense, but an estimated 700 officials were employed annually in the business of administration. There were market inspectors and assessors of weights and measures, whose job was to protect buyers of goods in the marketplace. City magistrates, helped by slaves, tackled tasks such as maintaining public buildings, policing the streets and removing rubbish. Ambassadors were dispatched abroad to defend the interests of Athens. Jurors had to be assigned to courts, and magistrates to offices.

Service as a juror was expected of all male citizens aged thirty or over. Athens had a system of courts known as *dikasteria*. The word from which it derived, *dikastes*, meant both juror and judge. This was a democracy without lawyers. No trained judges presided. The magistrates in charge were amateurs. Their one-year term of office, which they held only once in their lives, involved administrative functions, not matters of legal substance. The law was not seen as the Law, the special domain of a privileged class of legal experts. It was regarded simply as rules made and applied by jurors themselves. There was no written constitution to guide deliberation; delegates decided what was right and wrong in each case.

BANISHING THE DEMAGOGUES

It was through these arrangements that the citizens of Athens, when judged by our standards, had an acute sensitivity to crafty manipulation, both from inside and outside the assembly. In the absence of political parties and periodic elections, they experimented with many different ways of placing public checks and balances on the exercise of power. Consider the custom of *graphē paranómōn*, a procedure by which citizens, under oath, brought suits against proposed or actual laws that were allegedly based on rash decisions and in contravention of existing laws. Or *ostrakismos* (ostracism), a forerunner of modern methods to ensure limited terms of office to political incumbents. This was a tactic to block the rise of demagogues, plotters and tyrants by banishing unduly popular leaders from the city for ten years, if a minimum number of voters favoured the expulsion. The banished were given ten days to quit the city. The demagogue suitably named Hyperbolus was among them; in 416–415 BCE he was banished to the island of Samos, where several years later he was murdered, leading the assembly to put an end to the practice.

In its heyday, ostracism was a democratic method of defending democracy against democratic excess. The word itself meant 'judgement by shards', because shards or potsherds made from clay (*ostraka*), the cheapest available writing materials, were used as ballots to vote against would-be demagogues, those scheming citizens suspected of wanting too much power. Once a year, the assembly met to decide whether there were potential oligarchs in its midst – in effect, it was an unpopularity contest. If a majority of the quorum of 6000 decided there were, then a day and time was set, usually two months later, for a hearing before the assembly. Since it was in the interests of both the friends and opponents of the candidates for ostracism to show up – whoever ended up with the most votes lost – turnout at the second vote was usually high. The agora throbbed with nervous tension. To keep the assembly as calm as possible, discussion before the final vote was restricted. The contest concluded with the unusual custom of fencing off a large open area of the agora, where the final vote was taken. After casting their votes, citizens had to remain within the enclosure until the votes were counted and the name of the sacrificed was announced, to prevent fraud. It was one man, one vote, one victim.

Ostraka cast against Aristeides, Themistokles, Kimon and Pericles in Athens in the fifth century BCE.

THE ENEMIES OF DEMOCRACY

Looking back on the age of assembly democracy, it's clear that the advent of *dēmokratia* caused great commotions and almighty backlashes. This was, after all, a time in which politics was still dominated by propertied aristocrats locked in competition with each other, as well as with their democrat opponents. What this self-styled class of aristocrats had in common was their deep disgust for democracy. The word crossed their lips with a snarl. They loathed the assemblies. Whenever they heard talk of *dēmokratia*, it confirmed to them that Athens had taken a wrong turn, foolishly placed power in the hands of an ignorant and self-interested sectional group. This crazed *dēmos* was to be despised and feared. It was poor and property-less, ignorant and excitable. Worst of all, it was driven by a wolfish hunger for political power. They pointed out that the word *dēmokratia* meant manipulation, trickery and violence. Hence their conviction that it had to be given a bad name.

To understand their train of thinking, ponder for a moment the verb *kratein*. Nowadays it is usually translated (through the Latin word *regulare*) as 'to rule' or 'to govern', but that does damage to its original connotations, which were in fact much harsher. Strange as it may seem to us, when Athenians used the word they spoke the language of military manoeuvring and conquest. *Kratein* means to be master of, to lord over, to get the upper hand over somebody or something, to possess (in modern Greek the same verb means to keep or hold). The noun *kratos*, from which the compound *dēmokratia* was formed, referred to might, strength, a triumphant victory, especially through the application of force. The now-obsolete verb *dēmokrateo* brimmed with these connotations: it meant to democratise in the sense of grasping power and exercising control over others. So for some Athenians, and most certainly for its enemies, *dēmokratia* had the *opposite* meaning it has today.

In our times, when people speak positively of democracy, they typically mean free and fair elections, peaceful power-sharing through compromise, equality based upon legally guaranteed respect for others' dignity. For its Athenian foes, in striking contrast, *dēmokratia* was a menace. They treated it as a calamitous form of mob rule in which the lowbrow *dēmos* acts high-handedly in pursuit of its own interests; they insisted that the narrow preoccupations of the *dēmos* were not synonymous with the common good. The fact that democracy was depicted as a woman reinforced the point: in a *dēmokratia*, the *dēmos* holds *kratos* and so, much like a woman, it is prone to act deviously, to get its way by using trickery and force against its opponents.

In c. 387 BCE, outside the city walls of Athens, anti-democrat Plato founded a philosophical academy whose scholars mostly shared his view of dēmocracy as a disorderly and dangerous form of rule by the ignorant.

Violent shenanigans triggered by the lust for power were very much on Plato's mind when he remarked that democracy was a two-faced form of government, 'according to whether the masses rule over the owners of property by force or by consent'.[9] Democracy was for him a gimcrack invention that destroyed good government by pandering to the ignorant poor. He likened it to a ship manned by saphead sailors who refuse to believe that there is any such craft as navigation – idiots who treat helmsmen as useless stargazers. Switching metaphors, Plato even called it *theatrocracy*: the presumption that commoners are qualified to talk about everything, in defiance of immutable political laws, leads to posturing, the rhetorical seduction of the powerless, and lawlessness among the powerful. *Dēmokratia* is a type of fake government in which the people are ruled while seeming to rule.

Plato's view not only reminds us that Athenian philosophy was largely anti-democratic – something like a spiteful reaction against the ethos of equality, contingency and public openness nurtured by democracy. Since writing in philosophical ways about democracy required wealth, leisure and distance from the scuttle and fizz of political life, and since by contrast democracy required citizens to dedicate themselves to public life, the silence of the Athenian democrats about their own democracy enabled its octopoid enemies to squirt ink into its face. Efforts to silence democrats by polluting their reputation was the first recorded example of how democracy's enemies tried to destroy it – by robbing their opponents of their own language and trashing its practical achievements.

Since the friends of Athenian democracy either mistrusted or never used writing as an instrument of public expression, recorded history was forfeited to their opponents. That is why Athens produced no great theorists of democracy. It is also why virtually all the written commentaries on Athenian democracy were hostile to its novelty, especially to the way it stirred up public resistance to the rule of the rich. Democrats paid heavily for their unwritten defence. Firm believers in their own originality, convinced they had a goddess onside,

'Is there a democratic way of speaking about democracy?' asked Nicole Loraux (1943–2003), a scholar of classical Athens revered for her critical analyses of the enemies of democracy and her pioneering accounts of its myths, politics and gendered customs.

Athenian democrats underestimated the risk of their own obliteration, which is what nearly happened. In matters of memory, they put themselves at the mercy of a class of nobles that dreamed of crushing the ugly beetle of democracy underfoot. This class of amnesiacs had something sinister in mind: they wanted nobody to record for posterity what democrats had to say.

HUBRIS

The anti-democrats fought fiercely, with more than words, for which they were twice rewarded towards the end of the fifth century. During the Peloponnesian War (431–404 BCE), waged by Athens and its allies against Sparta, two coups d'état briefly interrupted democratic government. Both interludes were named for the number of conspirators who grabbed the reins of power: the Four Hundred (411 BCE) and the Thirty (404 BCE). Rearguard actions by men of property were to be repeated often in the story of democracy and, as in our times, they backed rogue governments favouring the rich. That's why Athenian democrats understood that when it comes to determining who gets how much, when and how, everybody should watch their backs. Politics produces losers, especially when some grow greedy for power. Athenian democrats were convinced that the deities would heap downfall and destruction, or *nemesis*, on kings, tyrants and lords who chased after worldly success and blindly gambled with their power, sometimes risking everything for the sake of gain. Hubris was their name for such gluttony. Ruin was said to be its penalty. Cupidity – the lust after money, fame, material goods or power – was stupidity.

This awareness of the dangers of arbitrary power prompted a troubling question for local democrats: would the deities turn a blind eye to the meteoric rise to power of a city-state that became an empire – the first-ever democratic empire?

By 450 BCE, Athens had no fewer than 160 vassal states. There was a robust sense among Athenians that they were superior to local states and to Asiatic peoples ruled by Persians. They regarded their democracy with pride. The reputation of Athens as a pompous busybody (*polypragmon*) constantly striving for power over others became synonymous with democracy itself. Consider Thucydides' famous account of the funeral oration delivered by Pericles at the beginning of the Peloponnesian War. 'For this land of ours, in which the same people have never ceased to dwell in an unbroken line of successive generations, they by their valour transmitted to our times a free state [and] the empire we now possess,' Pericles reportedly boasted.

> We live under a form of government which does not emulate the institutions of our neighbours; on the contrary, we are ourselves a model ... [O]ur government is called a democracy, because its administration is in the hands, not of the few, but of the many ... And our city is so great that all the products of all the earth flow in upon us ... We are also superior to our opponents in our system of training for warfare ... Wealth we employ rather as an opportunity for action than as a subject for boasting ... For we alone regard the man who takes no part in public affairs, not as one who minds his own business, but as good for nothing; and we Athenians decide public questions for ourselves or at least endeavour to arrive at a sound understanding of them, in the belief that it is not debate that is a hindrance to action, but rather not to be instructed by debate before the time comes for action ... In short, I say that our city as a whole is the school of Hellas.[10]

Talk of Athens as headmaster of the whole Greek world burned like dung in the fires of empire. It fostered public belief in the citizenly virtue of military prowess; it twinned *dēmokratia* with military success. Imperial power necessitated

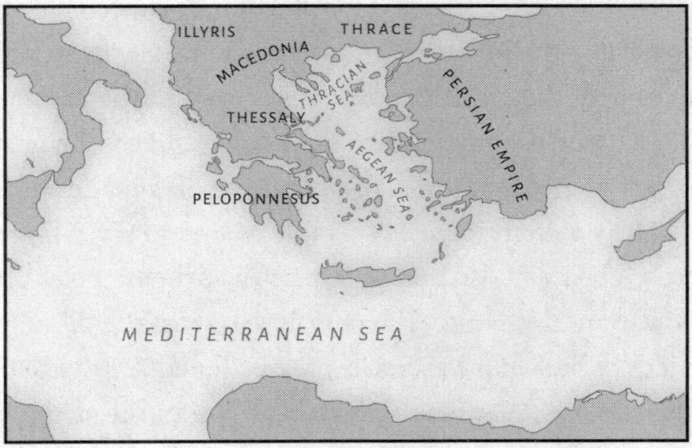

At its height in the mid-fifth century BCE, the Athenian Empire colonised important parts of the territory of modern-day southern Italy and the coastlines of Turkey, North Africa and the Middle East.

Pericles' famous funeral oration was delivered at the end of the first year of almost three decades of war between Athens and Sparta. 'When the bodies had been buried,' reported the historian Thucydides, 'Pericles, son of Xanthippus, climbed on a step, from where all the people could see and hear him, and gave this discourse.'

the mobilisation of troops – in return, they expected a share of government. The Athenian army had initially been largely self-funded: the wealthier citizens served in the cavalry on their own horses, mounted on their own saddles. The growth of lightly armed infantries of poorer hoplites made the case for political inclusion irrefutable. Democracy's logic of enfranchisement also meant that as the Athenian navy grew in power and influence, the poorest citizens, the *thetes*, who formed the bulk of naval crews, pressed for equality with their fellow citizens. War made everyone equal in the struggle to escape the clutches of death. It encouraged painful toil that produced honour. It confirmed men's sense of machismo (the Athenians spoke of *aretē*). It helped banish the cruel 'melancholy' Pericles mentioned in his funeral oration. War blessed life with unshakeable meaning; it helped men cast off worries that they were mere shadows of shadows, beings destined to endure only briefly, like a day passing into the night.

Empire also brought wealth to Athens, which was used partly to pay for its machinery of government and to conscript vast numbers of Athenian males. Save for a small number of states that negotiated to keep their nominal independence by providing ships that sailed in the Athenian fleets, by the early 440s BCE all cities of the empire were required to pay an annual tribute, as well as duties on exports and imports that passed through the hub port of Piraeus.

The extent to which the wealth generated by empire was vital to Athenian democracy's flourishing is still hotly disputed by historians. But there's little doubt that among the most potent effects of empire was to expand the power of the military in the day-to-day functioning of the polity. The Athenians were good democrats. They were also good fighters. In consequence, during the fifth century, Athens found itself at war on average two out of every three years; never once did it enjoy more than a decade of peace. With the introduction of paid military service in the 450s, war came to dominate the everyday lives of Athenians, as well as their culture and politics. Citizenship and military service grew indistinguishable; the spirit and institutions of democracy felt deeply martial.

DEMOCRACY'S DOWNFALL

Hindsight makes it clear that the dalliance of democracy and armed force proved fatal for Athens. The zenith of empire in the fifth century led to restrictions upon political freedoms at home. Empire bred demagoguery. It gave undue prominence to elected military leaders such as Kimon and Pericles, who (unusually) were entitled to hold office for several successive terms. These men of the battlefield were authorised to interrupt assembly proceedings to introduce their own business. That meant that their enormous power to determine the city's fate, unchecked by parties or laws, came to depend heavily on their skilful rhetorical massaging of the *dēmos*. Pericles cultivated his charisma by likening himself to Athens' courier ship, the *Salaminia*: while enjoying office for nearly a quarter of a century, from 454 to 429 BCE, he appeared before the assembly only when pressing public matters required urgent attention. His absence bred intrigue and excitement. Thucydides and others understandably complained that when he did appear in public, he spoke and acted like an arrogant monarch. 'Hatred and unpopularity have become the lot of all who have aspired to rule others,' Pericles said to mourners gathered to honour dead soldiers. But he added, defiantly:

> Remember, too, that if your country has the greatest name in all the world, it is because she has never bent before disaster; because she has expended more life and effort in war than any other city, and has won for herself a power greater than any hitherto known . . . it will be remembered that we held rule over more Hellenes than any other Hellenic state, that we carried out the greatest wars against their united or separate powers, and inhabited a city unrivalled by any other in its resources or magnitude.

The great leader's words presaged the beginning of the end of the Athenian experiment with democracy. Its decline was protracted; setbacks came camouflaged in victories. But growing militarisation of political life in support of empire began to turn Athens into its own worst enemy – into a source of envy and jealousy among the states within and beyond its empire. At home, it unleashed a malignant force that the Athenians called delusion (*ate*). A restrictive citizenship law passed in 451 BCE aimed to prevent foreign residents and freed slaves from becoming Athenian citizens; they were treated as the enemy within. On several occasions, every available citizen was compulsorily drafted into the navy or army to fight against a neighbouring city; and laws were passed by the assembly to enable citizenship to be stripped from those found guilty of desertion or draft dodging.

The ruinous compact between democracy and armed force had wider, geopolitical implications, with bad news for local democracies – such as the Aegean island of Melos, which was blockaded by Athens in 416–415 BCE. The siege had frightful effects. Starvation followed by discord and treachery resulted in the unconditional surrender of the Melians. The Athenian democrats wasted no time in pulling apart the local polity. In the name of democracy, they executed all men of military age and sold the women and children into slavery, leaving infants and the elderly to the local wolves. Five hundred citizen-settlers were soon shipped to Melos. The island became a colony of Athens. The rule of democracy was sealed, in cruelty and blood.

What were the lessons of the campaign against Melos? For a start, it showed that democratic states could be good at war, and capable of inflicting terrible violence upon neighbours. It proved, as well, that violence was a double-edged sword for Athens. Violence encouraged rivals to seek, and win, the ultimate prize: forcing Athens to its knees, where its hypocrisy and hubris were drowned in blood.

In 359 BCE, Athens was forced to submit to the well-armed kingdom of Macedon, led by Philip II. His giant army of 32,000 troops crushed the democrats and their allies at the Battle of Chaeronea, in Boeotia, to the north-west of Athens. The Macedonians soon tightened the noose around the necks of the Athenians, who in 322 BCE suffered another catastrophic defeat during the Greek-led rebellion against Macedonian rule, known as the Lamian War. Athens was forced this time to pay a much higher price. As part of the peace settlement, Macedonian troops stormed the city and promptly replaced its democratic government with an oligarchy. Somewhere between 12,000 and 22,000 citizens were disfranchised. Some were packed off to remote Thrace. Prominent democrats, among them Hyperides and Demosthenes, were executed.

Democrats regained control of Athens several times, but in the end the Macedonians would have nothing of it. In 260 BCE, the Macedonian king Antigonus Gonatas ordered his troops to recapture the city. The ideals and institutions of the most powerful assembly democracy of the ancient world were no more.

PART TWO

Electoral Democracy

IF THE HISTORY OF DEMOCRACY were a straightforward tale in which times changed but everything else remained the same, this short book would be nearing its end. For better, and not worse, the history of democracy isn't like that. So there should be no surprise that a startling upheaval in the story is about to happen, a change that produced a second historical phase of democracy. Let's call it the birth of electoral democracy.

Assembly democracy was born of the Near East and the Phoenician and Greek worlds. From around the twelfth century CE, democracy entered a new era whose centre of gravity was the Atlantic region – the watery geographic triangle that stretched from the shores of Europe, across to Baltimore and New York, and down to Caracas, Montevideo and Buenos Aires. It witnessed the birth of an imaginatively new understanding of democracy – as popular self-government based on the election of representatives who hold office and govern on behalf of the people, for a while. The region also witnessed the invention of many new institutions and customs – parliaments, written constitutions, political parties, polling stations, independent publishers and daily newspapers – designed to underwrite periodic elections. As we are going to see, electoral democracy aroused great public excitement and hopes among the downtrodden for a better-governed world cleansed of bossing and bullying. But it was dogged by internal contradictions and fierce opposition from its frightened enemies.

This lengthy period opened with the birth of parliamentary assemblies in northern Spain. It ended on a sad and sorry note, during the 1920s and 1930s, with the near-global destruction of representative democratic institutions by the bloody forces of war, revolution, dictatorship and totalitarian rule that racked the first half of the twentieth century. By 1941, there were fewer than a dozen electoral democracies left on our planet. In between, over the course of eight centuries, extraordinary things happened.

'GOVERNMENT DEMOCRATICAL, BUT REPRESENTATIVE'

How to make good sense of this long transition? Let's begin by consulting a salient letter written in the summer of 1816 by former US president Thomas Jefferson. Pondering the changes to government and political thinking during his lifetime, he minced no words: the arrival of electoral democracy had fundamentally altered the dynamics of the modern world. He explained that although the ancient Greeks knew nothing of the principles of electoral representation, the truth was the 'direct democracy' of the assembly required institutions of 'representation' that served to protect and to nurture the will of its citizens. According to Jefferson, it did not occur to the Greeks 'That where the citizens cannot meet to transact their business in person, they alone have the right to choose the agents who shall transact it'. Greek citizens, orators and political thinkers alike didn't see the possibility of breaking free from the false choice between self-government of the people and rule by a few – oligarchy.

The defining novelty of the modern era, Jefferson continued – America and Western Europe were foremost in his mind – was its invention of a new type of self-governing republic based on periodic elections. He made no mention of the disfiguring of elections by rum-soaked parades, vote buying, gun battles and riotous brawls, and said not a word of his slave-owner's conviction that a multiracial society with free black people was impossible. He instead concluded that the experiment in combining 'government democratical, but representative, was and is still reserved for us'. The new representative system had no historical precedent. It offered 'The people' a method of protection 'against the selfishness of rulers not subject to their control at short periods'. In providing such protection, the experiment with electoral democracy 'rendered useless almost everything written before on the structure of government'.[1]

The bold words raised big questions, to do with the tricky matter of when and how a new era had been triggered by inventions that invested the word 'democracy' with a brand-new meaning unknown to the Greeks. How did it come to be redefined as electoral democracy? How did it manage to take root on every continent? Why, in its European birthplace, did it ultimately fail as a political experiment? And most importantly, are the unique historical circumstances that gave rise to it now behind us – are we living in a world *beyond* the age of election-centred democracy?

THE LANGUAGE OF CHOICE

'Persons attempting to find a motive in this narrative will be prosecuted; persons attempting to find a moral in it will be banished; persons attempting to find a plot in it will be shot,' Mark Twain wrote in the preface to *The Adventures of Huckleberry Finn*. The story of the birth and development of electoral democracy is not exactly a Twainian mystery, but crooked and kinked its birth patterns certainly were.

Let's take an example that illustrates just how complicated are the origins of electoral democracy: the language of elections. By the early years of the nineteenth century, as Jefferson pointed out, 'free and fair' elections were thought to be the heart and soul of this new form of democracy. But the vocabulary of elections is a magpie's nest of different words with disparate origins. The word 'election' stems from the Latin 'To choose; to pick out [from among several possibilities]'. The group term for those who choose, the 'electorate', is much more recent; its first recorded usage dates only from 1879. Before then, the word that everybody used was 'electors'. The general entitlement to vote is nowadays called 'The franchise', but that word (in thirteenth-century English) originally meant 'privilege or right' and 'freedom, exemption from servitude or domination'. Talk of the franchise later came to refer to the legal immunity from prosecution, only then to evolve into several new meanings, including the act of granting a right or privilege (as when a sovereign monarch granted exemption from arrest), an 'elective franchise' (the right to vote) or, as in today's use of the word, a licence granted by a business to someone to sell or trade its products within a given area.

Then there are terms such as 'representative'. It comes from the Latin *repraesentare* –serving to portray, depict or display – but the later meaning of a representative chosen to act on behalf of others was quite possibly a gift from the world of early Islam, where the practice of appointing *wakīl* to handle distant legal, commercial and religious matters was customary (*wakīl* is also one of the names of God, meaning 'dependable'). And there is the word 'voting', from the Latin *votum*. It entered English during the fourteenth century to mean 'To wish or to vow' and 'To promise or dedicate', then was transformed in Scotland around 1600 to mean expressing a choice in an election. 'Poll' was also used to describe the act of casting a vote. In its old Dutch and Germanic origins – and in several surviving dialects – it meant 'head'. During the last years of the sixteenth century, it came to refer to the new custom of conducting a vote by head count, designed to put an end to the corrupt practice of elections being decided by those who shouted loudest in favour of their candidate. *That* word stems from the days of the Roman Republic, where the Latin *candidatus* meant 'clothed in white'. It referred to political men who dressed in white togas as part of their bid to become members of the governing and advisory assembly of the aristocracy known as the Senate.

The language of elections reminds us that the beginnings of electoral democracy are complex. It was not a straightforwardly 'modern' invention, as we often think, but had roots in medieval Europe. It was not primarily the offspring of the 'modernisation' processes analysed by academics, or born of 'the emergence and development of the modern

Election Night Bonfire (1928) captures what New York–based artist Glenn O. Coleman called the 'mad beauty' and the rough-and-tumble excitement aroused by working-class voting in an era dominated by political party bosses and fat-cat business donors.

nation-state', as scholar David Runciman suggests.[2] Nor was it the progeny of the eighteenth-century American Revolution, as political scientist Francis Fukuyama has claimed. It was neither the work of the aristocracy nor simply an expression of 'The rise of the bourgeoisie', or of liberalism, as was commonly thought by Karl Marx, Harold Laski, Carl Schmitt and other political writers who pondered the subject during the past two centuries. Multiple forces and events within the Atlantic region conspired to produce electoral democracy. It was often a child of unintended consequences, neither preordained nor inevitable. Its birth and survival, as well as its mutation and eventual collapse, defied simple formulae and universal laws. And fascinating is the way that several of its key institutions were never originally thought by their inventors to have anything to do with 'democracy'. Usually, they despised the word.

Many hands were responsible for crafting the institutions of electoral democracy. Monarchs, monks, shepherds, women, statesmen and aristocrats all played a part. So too did artisans, republicans, clergymen, moneylenders, city dwellers, farmers, soldiers, publishers, devout Muslims and God-fearing Protestant dissidents. Since it preserved, in its principles and its practice, the understanding of democracy as popular self-government – the right of voters to gather freely in public meetings, for instance – electoral democracy was also indebted to the ancient Greek world of assembly democracy.

Throughout the Atlantic region, there were red-hot disagreements over what exactly representation meant, who was entitled to represent whom, and what had to be done when representatives snubbed or frustrated those they supposedly represented. The merits of elected government were also hotly disputed. But what was common to this period was the growing awareness that government by elected representatives had a definite magnetism for millions of people convinced it could deliver them a better way of life.

REIMAGINING DEMOCRACY

Many centuries after the disappearance of democracy in Athens, assemblies continued to flourish at particular times and places throughout the Atlantic region. Public meetings known as *contiones* were convened regularly by the rulers of the Roman Republic, which survived until 27 BCE. Assemblies reappeared in the Faroe Islands and Iceland, where from around 930 a midsummer *al-thing* or *alping* convened annually; in the Swiss cantons, governed by citizens' assemblies variously called *landsgemeinde, talschaft* and *teding*; and in British American colonies such as Virginia, where the first assemblies dating from the early seventeenth century were attended and controlled by slave-owning Protestant men of wealth.

The inaugural session of the House of Burgesses, the first elected legislative assembly in the American colonies, in Jamestown, Virginia, 1619.

So the train of assembly-based democracy didn't simply terminate at one historical station, where passengers alighted, then boarded the next train of electoral democracy. There were breakthroughs, setbacks, dramatic upheavals and slow-motion ruptures. And more than a few moments when the early champions of periodic elections seemed not to grasp the long-term democratic significance of their doings.

A case in point is the invention of the phrase 'representative democracy'. The twinned words were first used towards the end of the eighteenth century by constitution-makers, political writers and citizens when referring to a new type of elected government founded on popular consent. What's not clear is who coined it. There's evidence that the oxymoron has Anglo-Dutch-French-American parentage. There are many odd moments when the phrase was spoken but neither its meaning nor its historic significance was understood by those who uttered it. Eighteenth-century Frenchman Charles-Louis de Secondat, Baron de Montesquieu (1689–1755), a modestly wealthy member of the Bordeaux aristocracy who served for a while as the deputy president of the Bordeaux *parlement*, pointed out in *The Spirit of the Laws* (1748) that in a democracy 'The people, in whom the supreme power resides, ought to have the management of everything within their reach', but 'That which exceeds their abilities must be conducted by their ministers'.[3]

Ministers? What did it mean to entrust the people's business to them? The French nobleman who had been foreign minister under Louis XV, the Marquis d'Argenson (1694–1757), was well placed to answer such questions. He was among the first writers to tease out both the meaning of the word and the new definition of democracy as popular representation. D'Argenson wrote of the difference between 'false' and 'True' democracy:

> False democracy soon collapses into anarchy. It is government of the multitude; such is a people in revolt, insolently

> scorning law and reason. Its tyrannical despotism is obvious from the violence of its movements and the uncertainty of its deliberations. In true democracy, one acts through deputies, who are authorised by election; the mission of those elected by the people and the authority that such officials carry constitute the public power.[4]

His unorthodox reasoning was that democracy needn't be feared because it wasn't mob rule. Little wonder his book was banned by the royal authorities and circulated clandestinely in manuscript form for three decades before its posthumous publication.

Others soon set about exploring and popularising the links between democracy and 'deputies ... authorised by election', and their contributions travelled across oceans and through whole continents – fast. On the other side of the Atlantic, James Madison (1751–1836), drafter of the new US Constitution and later president of the republic, expressed disdain for the word 'democracy' yet counted himself among those who saw the novelty of the American political experiment in 'The delegation of the government ... to a small number of citizens elected by the rest'.[5] Alexander Hamilton (c. 1755–1804) was perhaps the first American revolutionary to nudge the words 'representation' and 'democracy' together, even at one point using the brand-new phrase 'representative democracy', without understanding its historical significance. It's weird to think that some of the most precious terms in the history of democracy were coined as if in a dream, but so it was with Hamilton and the new phrase. He was normally hostile to popular rule, which he condemned as a formula for 'Tyranny' and 'deformity' led by 'an ungovernable mob'. Yet on one occasion, shortly after the Declaration of Independence, Hamilton denied that 'instability is inherent in the nature of popular governments'. Such governments, he said, could be 'happy, regular and durable' if they took the form of 'representative democracy, where the right of election is well secured and regulated and the exercise of the legislature, executive, and judiciary authorities is vested in select persons, chosen *really* and not *nominally* by the people'.[6]

The same point was made more bluntly by a fellow Scot, James Wilson (1742–1798), an erudite Presbyterian lawyer who also helped draft the 1787 Constitution. Wilson noted that the new federal constitution of the American republic was doubly unusual: it recognised that 'representation is made necessary only because it is impossible for the people to act collectively', in consequence of which the new republic was 'purely democratical', since 'all authority of every kind is derived by representation from the people and the democratic principle is carried into every part of the government'.[7]

These were blue-sky ways of rethinking democracy, which by now meant a type of government where voters, faced with a genuine choice between at least two alternatives, elected leaders who acted in their interests. Lord Henry Brougham's widely read account of the principles of representation put things clearly. 'The essence of representation,' wrote the Edinburgh-born parliamentarian known for his advocacy of free trade, the abolition of slavery and the enfranchisement of the middle classes, 'is that the power of the people should be parted with, and given over, for a limited period, to the deputy chosen by the people, and that he [sic] should perform that part of the government which, but for this transfer, would have been performed by the people themselves.'[8]

THE ROLE OF REPRESENTATION

Curious readers will ask: why was this new way of thinking about democracy as popular representation seen as a step forward, an improvement upon assembly democracy?

The standard response historians often give is that electoral democracy was a functional response to territorial imperatives – a practical solution to the problem of how to exercise power responsibly within large-scale territorial states and empires, in which great distances prevented citizens from meeting in face-to-face assemblies. The case for electoral democracy was much more compelling. Thomas Jefferson's insistence that under conditions of representative democracy 'There is a fullness of time when men should go, and not occupy too long the ground to which others have a right to advance'[9] is a vital clue to the ingenious argument made by late eighteenth- and nineteenth-century publicists, constitution-makers, journalists and citizens.

Jefferson in effect pleaded a case for electoral democracy centred on political leadership. Unlike monarchy and despotism, democracy requires guidance, inspiration and support from popular leaders when handling complicated political matters, he said. True leaders who lead because they get people to look up to them, rather than dragging people by the nose. Yet he quickly added that representative democracy keeps leaders grounded. It grants them the authority to govern, but it also puts them on trial, mocks them, makes jokes at their expense and threatens scoundrels with loss of office. It provides citizens with a way of ditching lousy leaders who tell lies, cheat, prevaricate, promise miracles or act like demagogues. Unlike unelected monarchs and power-hungry tyrants and despots, elected representatives hold office only temporarily. Representative government is thus a brilliant formula for peace, a way of avoiding civil war by creating space for political dissent and offering losers an olive

The Politician (1775), a satirical etching by John Keyse Sherwin, is based on a sketch by the English artist William Hogarth, whose shortsighted friend, the lacemaker and politician Ebenezer Forrest, is here portrayed absentmindedly setting fire to his hat while reading a newspaper.

branch: the hope of running again for office, the reassurance that there are no misfits in the polity.

Leadership on a leash was one thing. Another benefit of electoral democracy, its supporters claimed, was its recognition that social disagreements and conflicts are legitimate. The point was captured by Jefferson's close political friend Thomas Paine (1737–1809). 'Athens, by representation, would have outrivaled her own democracy,' wrote the author of the biggest-selling books of the eighteenth century, including *Rights of Man* (1791). He thundered in favour of 'representation ingrafted upon democracy' as a new type of government that allowed for disagreements. It rejected monarchy and its outdated belief in a unified body politic; it was superior to the 'simple democracy' of ancient Athens, whose *dēmos* was under constant pressure to seek harmony, to act as if social diversity and divisions of political opinion were an impediment to popular rule. Electoral democracy, in contrast, openly acknowledged the legitimacy of social divisions and competition among different political parties. It spurned the idea that disagreement was undemocratic, and that the body politic should be undivided and guided by the infallible will of an imaginary People. 'A nation is not a body, the figure of which is to be represented by the human body,' Paine explained, 'but is like a body contained within a circle, having a common centre, in which every radius meets; and that centre is formed by representation.'[10]

This was an excitingly fresh way of thinking about the opportunities and dangers of handling political power. It became the philosophical basis for periodic elections with multiple political parties. Multi-party competition, which first happened in the United States during the 1820s, was among the core inventions of the age of electoral democracy. Once denounced as dangerous 'factions' and 'conspiracies', political parties became living reminders that any body politic was materially divided by different opinions and interests. In this new equation, parties did more than mobilise votes. They expressed disagreements, formulated policies, promoted literacy, provided jobs and welfare for their supporters, and prepared representatives for holding government office.

Parties also helped guarantee that an electoral democracy would be an unusual type of polity in which non-governmental associations known as 'civil society' could flourish. The principle was thoroughly modern: through bodies such as businesses, trade unions, churches, taverns, restaurants, scientific associations and printing houses, ran the reasoning, civil societies provided space for citizens to band together to pursue and protect their interests, to live their different lives as free equals, at a distance from governments, which would be kept on their toes by citizens armed with the right to vote for the party representatives of their choice.

The insistence that 'the people' is never a homogenous body and that democracy cannot exist without means to represent differences in opinion was used by the early champions of electoral democracy to justify ridding the world of the hereditary stupidity of monarchs such as George III. Representative government attacked the fallacy that sperm, eggs and refined manners were the secrets of good government.

It instead supposed that, since political talk of 'The people' is a hollow abstraction, it is best to encourage the non-violent, public airing of different interests and opinions, handled by responsible leadership guided by the principles of good government laced with political compromise.

The eighteenth-century champions of representation also offered a pragmatic justification of their new type of government. Representative democracy was considered a remedy for the practical problem that not all citizens can be involved in making all the decisions that affect their lives, even if they have the time and means to do so. The principle that everyone who is affected by a decision has an inalienable right to be involved in forming and applying that decision was seen to be unworkable, too Greek. People must delegate the task of government to chosen representatives, so the argument ran. The job of these representatives is to monitor the expenditure of public money. They make representations to the government and its bureaucracy on behalf of their constituents. They debate issues and make laws. Governing on behalf of the people, they craft foreign policy. 'In its original state,' wrote Paine, echoing D'Argenson, 'simple Democracy was no other than the commonhall of the ancients. As these democracies increased in population, and the territory extended, the simple democratical form became unwieldy and impracticable.' But, by grafting representation onto democracy, 'we arrive at a system of government capable of embracing and confederating all the various interests, and every extent of territory and population'.[11]

THE FIRST PARLIAMENT

The leap of imagination was astonishing; Jefferson and Paine gave voice to an epochal change in the meaning of democracy, which raises the practical question of when and how electoral democracy happened. To find an answer, let's visit the twelfth century, at the moment of the birth of a core institution of electoral democracy: parliamentary assemblies.

Parliaments were a new type of governing body, a place for assembled representatives of various social interests, drawn from a wide geographical radius, to make laws. Where were they born? Contrary to some devoutly English accounts, which suppose that parliamentary assemblies were 'incomparably the greatest gift of the English people to the civilisation of the world',[12] parliaments were in fact an invention of what is today northern Spain, in a region defined by power struggles among Christian revivalists bent on militarily evicting Muslims from the lands of Islam. Momentum was provided by a bellicose address in 1095 by Pope Urban II (1088–1099) before a large crowd gathered at Clermont, a French town today famous for the chain of extinct volcanoes surrounding it. The text of the speech hasn't survived, but various chroniclers tell us that Urban attributed the impending disaster facing Christianity to God's punishment for human wickedness – and that he called upon his hearers to recover grace by fighting for the cross, in the name of Europe. What exactly was required to 'go forward in happiness and in confidence to attack the enemies of God' (these were his reported words) was left to the good judgement of Christian-minded princes. Among them was King Alfonso IX of León (1188–1230), a savvy young ruler who pioneered an effective way of snatching fields and towns from the Muslims of northern Iberia.

The first-ever parliament Alfonso IX convened was born of despondency. Many Christian communities living in northern Spain had understandably grown concerned about their future. The seventh century had seen the followers of the Prophet Mohammed conquer Syria, Palestine, Egypt and the North African coast. During the next century, Muslims advanced to the gates of Constantinople and, after conquering Spain, entered southern France. The ninth century saw the sack of Rome, and Saracen forces occupy Sicily and the coasts and foothills of southern Italy. Fears that Christianity might disappear altogether were compounded by the loss of Jerusalem, and by the sense that the Christian world was fraying at its African and Asian edges. Nestorian and Jacobite churches were cut off by the Saracens' occupation of much of Asia Minor – and then of Persia. The church in Abyssinia was similarly quarantined, while in Syria, Egypt and elsewhere, tens of thousands of Christians felt squeezed by the combined forces of what they saw as discriminatory taxation and contemptuous toleration by Islamic rulers.

So the stage was set for a Christian fightback, led by Alfonso IX. At the ripe age of seventeen, he donned the crown of a kingdom that was under intense military pressure, not only from neighbouring kingdoms, but also from the Moorish armies that had first begun swiping swathes of land 400 years earlier. Repeated invasions by these Muslim armies threatened to sap the whole fiscal base of Alfonso's kingdom. The old custom whereby Muslim governors contributed money to the Christian kings of the region, known locally as *parias*, had collapsed. New taxes had been imposed on the churches and towns, but these proved highly unpopular. Petitions began to pour in to the new king's officials.

Alfonso IX caught his realm by surprise by deciding to fight his way out of a tight corner by reconquering territory that he and many of his subjects considered rightfully Christian. Strapped for cash, he slapped taxes on all Christians in his realm. In the era before the slogan 'no taxation without representation', his court set about enlisting support. The prince's aim was to defend and expand his kingdom, even if that meant making political compromises that might dilute his kingly powers. The move he made was as improbable as it was astonishing: he formed a parliament of representatives.

Alfonso IX turned first to the local nobility, the warrior aristocrats committed to the preservation and expansion of their lands. Convinced that monarchs had the Christian duty to wage unending war against Muslim infidels, they were sure that success in war was not only a commandment of Pope Urban II, but also necessary to enhance their own power and bolster government by good Christian princes. Alfonso IX also saw that war required winning over the bishops of the Church, the estate that saw itself as the guardian of souls and spiritual protector of God's lands. With the region permanently besieged, and strategically vital towns such as León now resembling walled fortresses, Alfonso IX also sought to court wealthy citizens. Contemporary documents referred to them as *cives* or *boni homines*: 'good men' with a reputation for leadership that stemmed from their election as officers of town councils, called *fueros*. They were well placed to deliver to the king both townsmen trained to bear arms and much-needed cash.

The modern practice of parliamentary representation was born of this medieval triangle comprising nobles, bishops and moneyed citizens. It was in the former Roman town of León, in the spring of March 1188 – a full generation before King John's Magna Carta of 1215 – that Alfonso IX convened the first-ever *cortes*, as contemporaries soon christened it, using the local term both for counsellors who advise and serve a monarch and for the city where a king resides. Delegates from all three of the region's estates – men of war, religion and commerce – met within the sandstone cloisters of the magnificently modest church of San Isidoro.

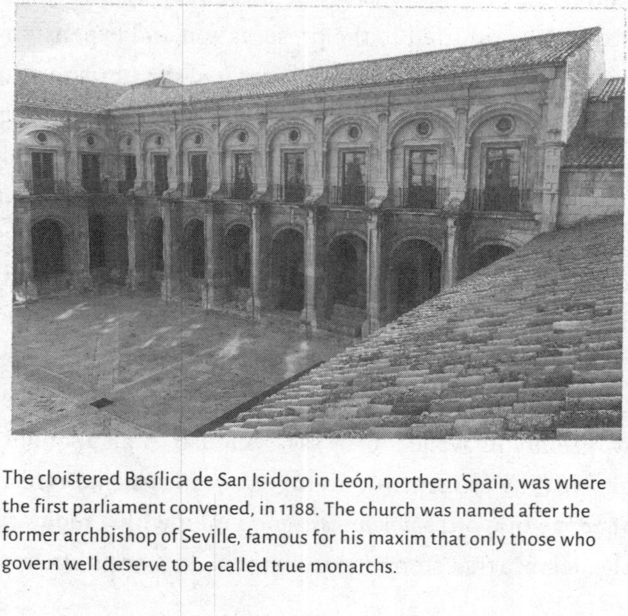

The cloistered Basílica de San Isidoro in León, northern Spain, was where the first parliament convened, in 1188. The church was named after the former archbishop of Seville, famous for his maxim that only those who govern well deserve to be called true monarchs.

The assembly wasn't the usual gathering of courtly sycophants. In fact, it was the first recorded convention of all three estates – the interests of the towns had hitherto been ignored in meetings convened by the region's monarchs. It produced up to fifteen decrees (the authenticity of several is disputed) that together amounted to something like a constitutional charter. The king promised that hereon he would consult with and accept the advice of the bishops, nobles and 'good men' of the towns in matters of war and peace, pacts and treaties. The bishops, until now forbidden to take oaths of allegiance to temporal power, joined the knights and town citizens in pledging that they too would work for peace and justice. The participants determined that property and security of residence were inviolable. They resolved that judicial proceedings and the laws they produced would be respected; and that the king's realm would be guided wherever possible by the general laws inherited from earlier times. It was also agreed that there would be future assemblies of the king and representatives chosen by the three estates.

REPRESENTATIVE GOVERNMENT

The good Christian representatives of the first-ever parliament could not have known their contribution to the coming age of electoral democracy. Yet the León assembly was of profound historical importance. Not only did it reject the old custom of courtiers meeting to reaffirm fealty to their sovereign's will; it also showed that political deals among conflicting interests could be struck by following the rules of fair play, without resorting to naked force or treating opponents as enemies. In stark contrast to Athenian democrats' belief that democracy could only function when citizens shared an undivided sense of political community, the *cortes* supposed the likelihood of competing and potentially conflicting interests, and the desirability of peaceful compromise among them. Moreover, it supposed that the chances of reaching workable agreements were improved by limiting the numbers of decision-makers – to perhaps several dozen representatives, though we can't be sure – some of whom were required to travel great distances from remote parts of the realm. Governments could govern without losing the trust and consent of their distant subjects, it affirmed, exactly because those involved in making decisions had the power to snap at the

Representatives of the three estates, later known as *procuradores*, considered themselves agents authorised to act on behalf of others, in defence of their group interests, in the presence of León's King Alfonso IX.

heels of the monarch, to defend the interests of their subjects, in the presence of the king.

This method of representative government soon became fashionable. It quickly took root elsewhere in northern Spain, where parliaments were especially active for the next three centuries.

These early parliaments weren't pushovers before power, mere gossip parlours or talk shops, as later critics of electoral democracy liked to quip. They handled common grievances, ranging from the conduct of war, relations with Muslims and Jews, and the environmental damage caused by the monarch's animals, through to forcible military recruitment, the appointment of ambassadors, standards of weights and measures, and the living conditions of the peasantry. Parliaments often seemed unafraid of making themselves a nuisance when monarchs tried to decide things arbitrarily, without regard for their subjects' wishes. Monarchs could rarely claim a grant (sometimes called a *servicio*) or impose taxes without their consent. Parliaments often collected taxes through their own agents and treasuries, prescribed how they should be spent and even demanded audits of the king's budget. Representative assemblies in rural areas meanwhile handled matters such as crop irrigation systems (the water tribunals of drought-prone Catalonia and Murcia are an example) and the allocation and coordination of cattle-grazing rights through mobile assemblies of shepherds called *mestas*. In these and other ways, parliaments served more than the interests of the dominant estates. They opposed arbitrary, arcane and violent rule, acted as a counterweight to petty tyranny and absolute monarchy, and, by stirring up demands for popular representation, nurtured the democratic spirit of 'liberty' and 'equality' commonly associated with later forms of representative government.

It's easy in retrospect to see the originality and long-term political impact of these new methods of representative government. Parliaments soon spread to other parts of Europe, migrated across oceans and helped give birth to a large family of institutions whose cumulative result was a wide variety of democracies in representative form. Some electoral democracies, as in Latin America and the United States, chose to rely on elected presidents exercising powers quite separate from their parliaments. Others, such as Greece, India and the Federal Republic of Germany, opted for parliamentary government with prime ministers or presidents directly answerable to the legislature. Canada, New Zealand and Australia instead chose parliamentary government headed by a monarch with largely ceremonial powers. There were highly centralised and federal systems of representative government, while some polities opted for highly decentralised systems of confederation, as in the newly independent republic of the United States and in Switzerland. Cities also proved important laboratories of representative self-government. Republican opposition to monarchy flourished in urban areas. So did local elections, city councils, independent judiciaries, *habeas corpus* (prohibitions upon torture and imprisonment) and, much later, elected governments that provided public transportation, parks and libraries for the use and enjoyment of their citizens. The point is that the book of electoral democracy lacked a consistent plot. There were many loose pages, odd paragraphs, a few completed but mostly unfinished outlines of possible themes. But amid all the clutter there was one common theme that lived on until the early decades of the twentieth century: democracy came to mean the self-government of people by representatives chosen in periodic elections.

As a practical way of handling power, electoral democracy proved that not everything turns full circle, and that new things do happen under the sun. It triggered great political disputes, centred on the thorny question of the meaning of representation. Lives were upended by revolutions. Blood was spilled. There were times, as in the early parliaments of northern Spain, when representatives broke the mandate of peaceful debate, fighting with fists and swords over two broadly conflicting definitions of representation. Were they mere servants and mouthpieces of their constituents, who needed to keep them on a short leash, or were they to be treated as free-spirited guardians of the whole political community? Should representatives have a set of carefully worded, binding instructions (*poderes*), forcing them to do as they were told? Was it best practice to give them a grilling when they returned from a session of parliament, as frequently happened in the Catalonian town of Barcelona, which used a permanent standing committee – *Vintiquatrena de Cort*, the Commission of the 24 – to keep tabs on its representatives' public and private lives? Were they sometimes obliged to say no to their constituents, to stand above the fray and work selflessly for the higher political good? If so, might unanimity on important measures be mandatory? Might consensus sometimes require the physical ejection of recalcitrants from parliament, kicking and shouting?

How sensible was the method used by the *cortes* of Aragon, which elected officers to vet representatives by putting them through a test, known as the *habilitacion*, designed to guarantee their commitment to unanimity? Was it true (as the local joke had it) that the passage of every law in Aragon was nothing short of a divine miracle?

THE CONSENT OF THE GOVERNED

Representative government produced moments of mirth, but it also gave birth to a large family of institutions and practices designed to handle the serious business of tempering governmental power. Among the most significant were written constitutions, of the kind agreed by the first parliamentary assembly in Léon. They came to be considered important means for protecting the principle of equality (of those who counted) under the law, restricting the hubris of governments claiming a popular mandate, and stopping seizures of power by an army or powerful political faction, such as the landowning aristocracy.

Within the sprawling body of Christian believers known as the Church, there were also councils and synods of representatives. Councils comprised church representatives meeting to discuss matters of faith and order, and to issue decrees in spiritual and earthly matters. Easily the most spectacular was the Council of Constance, an assembly of representatives that began in November 1414 in the imperial city of Constance, in Swabia (a southern region of present-day Germany). It lasted four years and attracted huge crowds of Christians and other witnesses to its proceedings. Convened by the king of Hungary, Sigismund of Luxembourg, the 600-strong council was tasked with resolving a rather serious problem. The Church was split by the existence of no fewer than three popes – John XXIII, Gregory XII and Benedict XIII – who each claimed exclusive title to the head of the Church. The question was: how on earth could the worldly trinity be combined into one? The council acted like a latter-day constitutional convention or a political party conference. Delegates agreed to elect a pope, but on the condition that further meetings took place, because the council derived its authority directly from Christ – so the pope's powers were only held on trust, for the benefit of the Church. The council was adamant: the Supreme Pontiff was the minister, not the sovereign, of the Church. His government rested upon the consent of the governed.

Scholars, bishops and cardinals debating with Pope John XXIII – the winner of the pope-off – at the Council of Constance, held during the years 1414–1418.

The principle that earthly power requires the consent of the faithful later resurfaced in the covenant movement championed by Protestant Calvinists in the Scottish lowlands and highlands during the sixteenth century. It was among the weightiest inventions in the history of electoral democracy. Note how so many of its basic institutions were marked by the cross. 'The democratic movement is the heir of the Christian movement,' remarked the nineteenth-century anti-philosopher Friedrich Nietzsche (1844–1900).[13] He was right. The whole idea of a covenant was based on the conviction that God is the source of all things human, the great watchman who looks unkindly on mortals who dare act as His substitute. 'Think on this and reflect: he who resists power resists God' were the words famously used by Ivan the Terrible (1530–1584) to justify absolute obedience to rulers, regardless of their stupidity or cruelty. The covenanters wanted nothing of such power-hungry poppycock. That's why they called on the faithful to band together with fellow believers to rein in earthly rulers who supposed they were divine. A seventeenth-century Glasgow preacher and supporter of a national covenant signed by 60,000 people from all walks of life, Alexander Henderson (1583–1646), used words in a sermon that would soon scare tyrants and fuel more than a few political revolutions: 'Whenever men begin to go out of line, forget their own subordination, then those that are under them become no way subject to them, because they go out of the right order.'[14]

Similar reasoning fuelled the fight for press freedom, the principle that citizens should refuse to let their state representatives claim exclusive control over printing presses.

Liberty of the press was initially justified in Christian terms, for instance in John Milton's *Areopagitica* (1644), which crafted the clever argument that the resilience of faithful believers must be daily tested by the words of the devil, circulated through books, newspapers, novels and pamphlets. Press freedom later became a core demand in the secular struggle for civil and political liberties, especially the right to vote. The demand first took root in the northern and western regions of Europe, including Ireland and the British Isles, from where it subsequently spread to the American colonies, Upper Canada and throughout Spanish America.

Parliaments, written constitutions, councils of representatives, liberty of the press: none of these institutions was known to the ancient world of assembly democracy. That's true as well for voting in periodic elections. The custom of raising hands, placing stones in a pot or handing in *ostrakia* were common in the ancient assemblies, but voting was not understood as an act of representation. Choosing representatives in free and fair periodic elections stood at the core of the new bundle of institutions called electoral democracy. Yes, voting for representatives had deep and tangled roots, extending back to the early Spanish parliaments and to power struggles within the medieval Christian Church. Yet when revisiting the history of elections, especially from the eighteenth century, it is hard to miss the novelty of the blood, sweat and tears invested in the historic life-and-death struggles for 'one person, one vote'.

The universal franchise was the great utopian energiser of early modern democratic politics. Passionate tracts and thrilling poems were written in its honour. Walt Whitman's 'Election Day, November, 1884' lionised American elections as the 'choosing day', a 'swordless conflict' and 'scene and show' more powerful than the thunderous falls of Niagara and the mighty Mississippi. The universal franchise and free elections aroused great expectations of uncorrupted and affordable government, political equality, social dignity and even the collective harmony of a classless society. Australian-born Muriel Lilah Matters (1877–1969), the first woman to speak in the British House of Commons – from the public gallery, chained to its railings – was sure of its public cleansing effects. Emily Pankhurst and other suffragettes were among those who predicted it would bring about the end of militarism. 'The ballot is as essential to democracy as the bayonet is to despotism,' wrote Walter Thomas Mills (1856–1942), the American socialist publisher and co-founder of the United Labour Party in New Zealand. 'Majority rule is the only rational method of administering the affairs of a free state. The elective franchise must be universal. It must be given on equal terms to all who share in the advantages and bear the responsibilities of living within the borders of such a state.'[15]

More than a few people sacrificed their lives for the principle and practice of uncorrupted elections, among them Francisco Madero (1873–1913), a Mexican democrat with a difference. A wealthy landowner with a social conscience, he was sure that representative democracy could not be imported into Mexico; it was not a purchasable commodity, or a weapon that could be packed in soldiers' backpacks and discharged through the barrel of a gun. Democracy was a sensibility. It had to come

Aiming to lift the spirits of the campaign for women's suffrage in Britain, Muriel Matters hired an airship to drop pamphlets over London on 16 February 1909, the day King Edward VII officially opened parliament. The underpowered 80-foot airship, with Matters seated in its basket, was blown off course by adverse winds and never reached Westminster, but the daring act generated considerable publicity for the cause, which finally succeeded in 1928, when women in England, Wales and Scotland received the vote on the same terms as men (over the age of twenty-one).

from the hearts of citizens. That is why Madero worked tirelessly to alter perceptions of power, building a citizens' network that campaigned for free and fair elections, and for the departure of Mexican dictator Porfirio Díaz. Electoral democracy demanded a radical change of mind, body and soul, Madero told his supporters. The apostle quit smoking, destroyed his private wine cellar, abandoned siestas and stopped eating meat; at one point, partly to escape the swelling crowds greeting him with '*Viva!*', he spent forty days and forty nights in the desert, under the Milky Way, near a ranch he called 'Australia'.

For Madero, the personal was political. That conviction blessed him, as it would later bless millions of citizens and their chosen representatives, with a profoundly felt faith in the democratic cause, and in the power of magnanimous leadership. 'Neither poverty, nor prison, nor death frighten me,' he wrote.[16] Madero's faith was rewarded by his election to the presidency with a nearly 90 per cent majority; at thirty-seven, this made him one of Mexico's youngest leaders. Just two years later, he was rewarded again with a bullet through the neck in the middle of the night – courtesy of a plot co-organised by the American ambassador, Henry Lane Wilson.

RESISTANCE AND VICTORIES

Demands for the universal franchise brimmed and bubbled with democratic spirit throughout the Atlantic region, but its opponents grew frightened. 'Democracy' was for them a dirty word. Nicholas Oresme's famous French translation of Aristotle's *Politics*, commissioned for court use by Charles V around 1370 and eventually printed in 1489, contains an illustration whose right (angelic) side includes monarchy, aristocracy and timocracy – rule by a wealthy propertied class guided by honour. Its left (devilish) side contains images of tyranny, oligarchy and democracy. Democracy is symbolised by commoners and soldiers, and by a half-dead victim slumped in a pillory.

Three centuries later, shortly after French Jacobins executed Louis XVI, democracy was given similar rough treatment by the leading English satirist James Gillray (1756–1815).

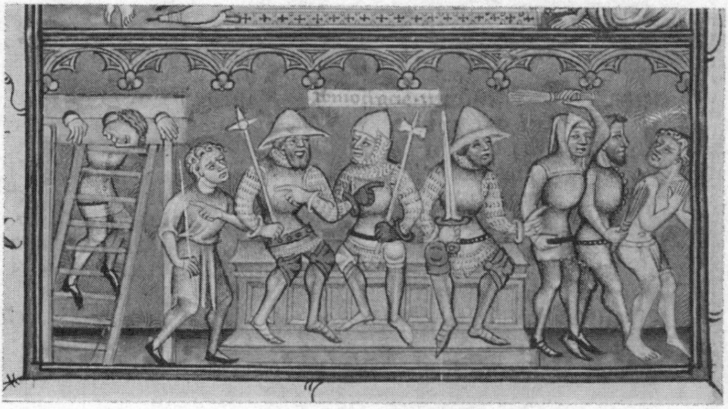

Democracy as recklessly violent government in Nicholas Oresme's fourteenth-century French translation of Aristotle's *Politics*.

Democracy is a bug-eyed, mouthy ruffian, a hirsute plebeian wearing a French cockade, a bloody dagger tucked in his belt, passing gas. Well into the nineteenth century, the iconography remained the same. For its sworn enemies, democracy was a synonym for rabbles of beasts, foul-smelling and rough-talking commoners dressed in rags, spreaders of ignorance and untamed passions, fomenters of chaos and class violence.

There was plenty of talk of democracy as properly the possession of the 'white race', as in the treatise *Die Demokratie von Athen* by the Hungarian historian and politician Gyula (Julius) Schvarcz (1839–1900).[17] The suggestion that folks of different wealth, race and gender were entitled to be treated equally within a political community, no matter its size or composition, bred snap and snarl. Long-serving Cornell University president Andrew White (1832–1918) warned that most potential voters were 'not alive even to their own most direct interests' and that the universal franchise would hand power to 'a crowd of illiterate peasants, freshly raked from Irish bogs, or Bohemian mines, or Italian robber nests'.[18] Mobilising the language of hostility to foreigners, women, the lower class and inferior races, Charles Francis Adams Jr, the grandson of John Quincy Adams and great-grandson of John Adams, similarly cautioned that, in the American context, 'universal suffrage

James Gillray's *A Democrat, or Reason & Philosophy* (1793) was completed shortly after Louis XVI's guillotining, the French declaration of war on Britain and the Dutch Republic, and the spread of revolutionary violence and terror in Paris. The democrat (based on local opposition leader Charles James Fox) is portrayed as a crazed sans-culotte celebrating the execution of the king and singing the revolutionary anthem 'Ca Ira' ('All Will Be Well'): *'All will be well, all will be well! / We'll have no more nobles or priests. / The aristocrats will swing from the posts. / And equality will reign in the streets.'*

can only mean in plain English the government of ignorance and vice – it means a European, and especially Celtic, proletariat on the Atlantic coast, an African proletariat on the shores of the Gulf, and a Chinese proletariat on the Pacific'.[19] Down south in Buenos Aires, Paul Groussac (1848–1929), the French-born conservative master of Argentine letters, playwright and head of the national library, denounced 'levelling democracy' as a recipe for 'moral regression' and barbarism. And elsewhere in Spanish America, more than a few well-placed public figures sided with the famous remark by Venezuelan soldier and strongman Simon Bolívar (1783–1830) that he felt in the marrow of his bones only an 'able despotism' could successfully rule the peoples of Spanish America.[20]

On the other side of the Atlantic, the founding statement of the German Conservative Party – drafted in 1876 by party leader Otto von Helldorff-Bedra with the help of a fellow Otto, Bismarck – warned against 'The increasing degeneration of the masses'. Universal suffrage was demonic; what was needed was a political order based on monarchy, a strong state, 'ordered' economic freedom and what it called the 'natural groups and organic divisions of the people'. Just across the North Sea, the famous historian of law Henry Sumner Maine's feistier insistence that the one-person, one-vote principle was a drag on progress was widely cited. 'Universal suffrage,' he wrote, 'would certainly have prohibited the spinning-jenny and the power-loom. It would certainly have forbidden the threshing-machine. It would have prevented the adoption of the Gregorian Calendar; and it would have restored the Stuarts.'[21]

Gruff words, vinegar sentiments, but historical trends proved more beneficent. By the early decades of the twentieth century, opposition to the one-person, one-vote principle was tempered, gradually worn down and defeated politically in the Atlantic region. Efforts to help citizens to better control and improve the quality of their chosen representatives blossomed. The dangers posed by majority rule ('The tyranny of a multitude is a multiplied tyranny', snapped the Anglo-Irish conservative writer and politician Edmund Burke[22]) and the merits of proportional representation were recognised. So was boycotting, an Irish invention. Political energies were invested in ridding elections of the corrupting effects of hand-in-the-air balloting, voter intimidation and pork-barrel bribery. The secret ballot – usually called the Australian ballot, as it was imported from the state of Tasmania – proved popular in places as far apart as Dublin, Salem, Boston, Caracas and Montevideo. The practice involved printing ballots containing the names of all candidates, distributing these at well-policed polling places, and requiring voters to mark them in secret and place their preferences in a sealed box, after which they were counted by officials, who were sworn to political neutrality.

American democrats pushed electoral innovations. They concentrated on reforms such as the direct election of senators (rather than appointing them via states and legislatures). The first breakthroughs happened in the states of Oregon and Nebraska, and soon after triumphed at the federal level in 1913, with the ratification of the Seventeenth Amendment to the Constitution. It was trumpeted as a great victory, the people's deserved triumph over the ailing system of state-appointed senators that had been adopted at the 1787 Constitutional Convention, partly on the spurious ground that slave-owning senators elected for longer periods by state legislatures would be gentleman representatives insulated from the selfish people of their own states.

The young American democracy also experimented with recall mechanisms designed to get rid of charlatans and blunderers. A champion of such innovations was doctor-turned-property-developer John Randolph Haynes, who led the Direct Legislation League of Los Angeles. He saw himself as a defender of 'The mass of citizens' rendered 'helpless between elections', and in speech after speech deplored 'inefficiency, extravagance and corruption'. He and his supporters managed to win approval for the inclusion of a recall clause in the Los Angeles city charter of 1903. At the state level, Oregon was the first to adopt the same measure, in 1908. Seventeen more states soon followed. In every case, the working principle was: if a sizeable number of citizens (usually between 10 and 40 per cent) were unhappy with the performance of their duly elected representatives in between elections, these representatives could be recalled before their terms expired. It was a way of giving a boot in the backside of dud politicians, who were either removed from office or allowed to complete the original term as if on a suspended sentence.

Americans also experimented with a modern version of the ancient Greek rule that citizens can initiate laws or amendments by referendum. In 1898 in the state of South Dakota, this rule had strong support within the trade unions as a valued weapon in the arsenal of what was called 'a people's legislation'. Progressives never managed to codify the initiative federally, but the referendum did come to be adopted widely at the state, county and local levels throughout the country. During the twentieth century, it was used by a remarkably wide spectrum of interests for different purposes, such as the enfranchisement of women, the abolition of the death penalty and the establishment of an eight-hour working day on public works projects (all this happened in Oregon). It came in two forms. The 'indirect initiative' specified that voters were mandated to submit petitions to the legislature for action. The more common 'direct initiative' specified that any matter could be drafted by any voter, but required the signature of usually between 5 and 15 per cent of registered voters before it could be put on the ballot, either at the next scheduled election, or at an election called especially to consider the proposition.

STATES AND EMPIRES

Referenda and recall, liberty of the press, periodic elections, political parties and parliaments: these institutions and the ways of thinking they promoted were both effective and unprecedented. Put paradoxically, electoral democracy fundamentally altered the history of democracy. It did so by proving that democracy could come to have two quite different, if entangled, meanings backed by different languages, different ways of thinking and different sets of institutions. The new politics of 'government democratical, but representative' also transformed the political geography of electoral democracy.

As time passed, and despite its localised origins in towns and villages, businesses and religious bodies, electoral democracy came to exist mainly within bordered, territorially defined states backed up by standing armies and law-making and taxation powers. That's why today we habitually speak of 'democracy in France', or 'South African' or 'Chilean' democracy. These states are qualitatively bigger and more populous than the political units of assembly democracy. Most democratic states of the Greek world – Argos and Mantinea, for instance – were no bigger than a few score square kilometres.

Empires also played a strange but interesting role in transforming the political geography of democracy. The thought that empires could hatch democratic innovations seems far-fetched, if not oxymoronic. After all, the two little words 'democracy' and 'empire' aren't happy family members, or even friendly neighbours. Electoral democracy: a form of polity in which power relations are regarded as contingent and permanently in need of checking and humbling through periodic elections. Empire: a jumbo-sized state whose economic, cultural, political and military powers extend well beyond its borders, and whose diverse lands and peoples are controlled by an emperor or imperial ruling group. Those who rule empires claim universal jurisdiction over their subjects based on such criteria as religion, race, tradition or 'civilised' manners. They back up their claims, ultimately, by their monopoly over the means of wealth extraction, cultural production, administration and violence. In other words, empires are dominant powers whose rulers are prone to rank themselves as superior to all their rivals combined. Imperial thinking was on display in the motto 'AEIOU' ('Austria is ruler of the whole world'), used by Frederick III (1415–1493) and other monarchs of the Habsburg Empire. As we have seen, Pericles had something similar in mind: the strength of democratic Athens, he said at the beginning of the Peloponnesian Wars, lay in her possession of naval forces more numerous and efficient than those of the rest of Hellas.

Imperialist mindsets help explain why empires developed a bad name, especially in modern democratic circles, where the word is dogged by charges of arrogance, resource greed and the domination and murder of peoples. This anti-democratic reputation is warranted. And yet, modern empires aren't cut from the same cloth. During the age of electoral democracy, three different types of empires made their mark on the world. Like the twentieth-century Soviet empire, some set out to crush all opposition and all the trimmings and trappings of electoral democracy by exercising ruthless centralised control over their subjects. There were empires that combined centralised control with substantive power-sharing with their subjects, for instance, the Ottomans' use of consultative assemblies (*meshwerets*) or the Austro-Hungarian rulers' reliance on a bicameral parliament known as the Reichsrat (Imperial Council). And then there were empires that functioned, despite their violence, greed and vanity, as midwives of electoral democracy.

Consider the British Empire: following the loss of its American colonies, nineteenth-century British government officials used a mix of three different types of governing strategies that marked their empire and its 'colonial possessions' with tessellated qualities. There were Crown colonies, such as Bechuanaland (today's Botswana) and Sarawak (a state of Malaysia), in which the empire granted little or no local say in matters of legislation, with administration carried out by public officers reporting to Westminster. There were colonies, such as India, which were granted representative institutions but prohibited from self-government because the Crown doubted they were ready. And, following the imperial rule that distant colonies functioned with least trouble when they were granted a measure of self-government, there were trusted dominions, granted both representative institutions and the power to govern, subject only to the Crown's veto on legislation and Westminster's control over the colonial governor.

It was in this last group of (typically white-dominated) colonies that impressive – by the standards of the day – innovations took place in electoral democracy. In 1791, a local house of assembly was granted in French-speaking Québec, then a British colony known as Lower Canada. A year later, free elections were held, based on a rule that enabled anyone who had reached the age of twenty-one to vote, so long as they owned property or paid annual rents and hadn't been convicted of treason or a serious criminal offence. The upshot was that all tenants – male or female, French- or English-speaking – paying the modest minimum annual rent of £10 were enfranchised. Large numbers of women voted, for the first time anywhere in the British Empire – 136 years before all women over twenty-one in Britain gained full voting rights. Women's right to vote was only temporary. It was legally abolished after Confederation (1867), but during the election of 1820 in the town of Trois-Rivières, a local judge, noting that 'here women vote just as men do, without discrimination', reported that a man entered the polling place only to be told that he could not vote because his property was in his wife's name. Red-faced, he was ordered to bring her to the polls, since she was the qualified voter in their family.[23]

War has often been a catalyst of democratic breakthroughs, and so it was for Canada's 'Bluebird' nurses stationed overseas during World War I. These women, serving at the Ontario Military Hospital in Orpington, England, in December 1917, were among the first to vote legally in a federal election since Confederation. All Canadian women won full voting rights the next year, after decades of petitioning, public rallies and acts of civil disobedience.

THE SOVEREIGN PEOPLE LEGEND

When looking back at these extraordinary developments, it's safe to say that the citizens of assembly democracies would have been puzzled by the novelty and scale of electoral democracy, even dumbfounded by its appearance. 'Ever since the birth of modern societies,' the nineteenth-century French liberal author and politician François Guizot (1787–1874) told a Paris audience during a famous course of public lectures on the subject, 'Their condition has been such that in their institution, in their aspirations, and in the course of their history, the representative form of government ... has constantly loomed more or less distinctly in the distance, as the port at which they must at length arrive, in spite of the storms which scatter them, and the obstacles which confront and oppose their entrance.'[24] Only doctrinaire liberal believers that history was on their side could have thought so optimistically about the future of representative government. In reality, things never went smoothly. Its champions were dogged by double standards, especially when they blocked women, slaves and the labouring classes from the gateways to government.

Outpourings of frustration were understandably widespread. Nineteenth-century novelist George Eliot (1819–1880) sarcastically likened elections to ceremonies of public deliberation and disappointment, with the catharsis of ticking and crossing before the slaughter of the result. 'Universal peace is declared,' she wrote, 'and the foxes have a sincere interest in prolonging the lives of the poultry.' Not only did periodic elections generate bitter resistance and disaffection; in places as different as France and Argentina, electoral democracy was also vulnerable to pathologies of its own making – flaws that dented its self-confidence and lifted the spirits and gritted the teeth of its enemies.

The champions of electoral democracy saw it as a means to admit differences of opinion and apportion blame for bad political leadership. It enabled citizens to complain publicly and let off steam about their leaders. It promoted open competitions for power, and it made room for tripping up whole governments and throwing them from office, if and when they failed, as surely they would in the end.

But let's pause to attend to this unusual feature of electoral democracy: the way its plea for multi-party pluralism contradicted and debunked the idea of a unified Sovereign People. Electoral democracy encouraged citizens and their elected representatives to cast doubt on the belief that there existed a unified body called 'The people' – a *dēmos* – that is the supreme source of worldly political power and authority. More than a few advocates of representative democracy, Thomas Jefferson among them, correctly spotted that this notion of the Sovereign People – which owed much to the ancient Greek world and something to Roman law and had its immediate roots in late medieval and early modern Europe – was actually a weird riff on the doctrine of the divine right of monarchs, the belief that kings and queens enjoy a God-given right to rule their subjects. The Sovereign People idea was a case of what anthropologists call animism: an instance of humans projecting onto the world their belief in an imagined God and then supposing that 'The people' were gifted and graced by this God to rule. It indulged the fantasy that 'The people' are the singular constituting power – the *pouvoir constituant*, as French thinkers described it. It turned 'The people' into a potential tyrant. *Vox populi, vox dei*: the voice of the people is the voice of God.

Listen for a moment to the words of the great American republican John Adams. The queue of adjectives he formed when analysing 'The people' was normally reserved by his fellow New Englanders for when they spoke of God: 'All intelligence, all power, all force, all authority,' he wrote, 'originally, inherently, necessarily, inseparably, and inalienably resides in the people.'[25] That way of speaking, suitably distilled for public consumption, was to reappear as 'We, the People', the first three words of the American federal constitution adopted in Philadelphia in mid-September 1787. The words confirmed that 'The people' are the rightful animators of the world. They call the shots. They cannot be contradicted. The People are power beyond morality. They know what is right and what is wrong. They know how things must be.

The defenders of electoral democracy cast opprobrium on simple-minded formulations of a magical people blessed with magical power – though they didn't put it in exactly this way. In effect, they issued a call to abandon the grand abstraction of 'The people' so that diverse flesh-and-blood peoples could live together and govern themselves well. But matters were messy. Most champions of electoral democracy continued to cling to the belief that 'The people' is a handy fiction in those moments when the enfranchised population, despite their differences of background and opinion, make an appearance as the 'sovereign' force. At election time, voters cast judgement on their representatives, sometimes harshly; 'The people' confer praise and applaud wildly, or they grow angry and vent their frustrations loudly. That followed from the principle, Benjamin Franklin said when debating the wording of the new constitution of the United States, that in 'free Governments, the rulers are the servants and the people their superiors and sovereigns'.[26] In between elections, 'The people' would resemble a dormant colossus, looking on with interest, all eyes and ears, mainly in silence, waiting for the next opportunity to pass judgement on those they elected to govern them for a while.

The upshot was that electoral democracy expressed two contradictory interpretations of 'The people': an abstract, imaginary Sovereign People deemed the rightful foundation of good government, and a real, actual populace shaped by diverse tastes and party competition and a variety of interest groups dwelling within civil society. From the end of the eighteenth century, when people first began speaking about representative democracy, this contradiction caused endless trouble, but electoral democracy nevertheless did what assembly democracy never managed to do. It challenged a metaphysical principle – the Sovereign People – that belonged to monarchist and absolutist ways of thinking. We could say that electoral democracy began the process of democratising the belief that democracy is essentially the rule of the sovereign people. It did so in a way unknown to the ancients.

Here's how: for electoral democrats, elections were much more than a method of choosing leaders or a means to periodically cheer up the disappointed with an opportunity to get rid of rogues and rascals. Elections remind citizens that they're members of a disunited 'people'. If decisions were always unanimous, and representatives always virtuous, impartial, competent and fully responsive to their constituents, elections would simply lose their purpose. Voters and their representatives would be mere mirrors of each other. Representation would become a meaningless principle; and political conflicts fuelled by the disjunction between what 'is' and what 'can be' or 'ought to be' would wither away. But since people aren't always in agreement and representatives aren't angels, and since in the eyes of the represented they never quite get things right and often get them badly wrong, elections are a vital means of disciplining them for having let down their electors. Through elections, the friends of representative democracy concluded, electors – a fictional body called 'The people' who in reality rarely see eye to eye about public and private matters – get their chance to remove representatives from office, and to replace them with substitutes who get on with governing, but only for a limited period.

POPULISM

This political reasoning stirred up public trouble. Bitter disagreement about electoral methods and fury at elected representatives plagued electoral democracy. As a new historical form of democracy, it also provoked serious dispute about the exact meaning of 'The people'. Compared with assembly democracy, electoral democracy called into question the belief that good government must be based on the unanimous or near-unanimous opinion of a body of people meeting face-to-face. This new type of democracy certainly preserved the old tradition of popular assemblies in town-hall meetings, political party rallies and public demonstrations. But what was also new about electoral democracy was its insistence that, for reasons of diversity and distance, 'The people' could not regularly assemble, and therefore they had to govern through their elected representatives backed by political parties operating within civil society.

Las Masas (The Masses), by the celebrated Mexican muralist José Clemente Orozco (1883–1949), is an ambivalent portrayal of popular sovereignty where 'the masses' of workers and peasants resemble a new headless force, with multiple eyes and mouths, feet and hands, a flag-waving people mobilised against an implicit enemy. The 1935 image recalls the violence that erupted at the beginning of the 1910 Mexican Revolution, which claimed the lives of up to 1.5 million people and forced several hundred thousand into exile.

Hard-line believers in the Sovereign People doctrine found this new formula objectionable. The trouble was this: when measured by the oft-quoted definition of democracy as 'government of the people, by the people, for the people' (the words famously used by Abraham Lincoln at Gettysburg to honour soldiers who perished in the American Civil War), electoral democracy was a dud. It promised government based on the principle that 'The people' are ultimately 'sovereign', yet in practice did the opposite. Not only did it condone the tearing apart of 'The people' by bickering, self-interested, divisive political parties and parliaments; electoral democracy was a formula for handing power to elected leaders who push aside 'The people' by speaking and acting on their behalf and consulting them directly just once in a while, during elections. Only then, in the lonely hour of the last instance, were 'The people' entitled to have the final say in determining who governs. Electoral democracy wantonly dishonoured the principle *vox populi, vox dei*. It offered a recipe for disappointment: the triumph of the will of elected representatives over the views and interests of people robbed of their sovereignty.

It comes as no surprise that with the spread of competitively fought elections, first in churches and cities and later within whole states and empires, electoral democracy was regularly plagued by populist outbursts. Ancient assembly democrats worried themselves sick about demagoguery, but populism, a word coined only in the mid-nineteenth century, turned out to be a serious autoimmune disease of electoral democracy. Demagogues promising the earth and acting in the name of 'The people' became commonplace. They helped stir up hopes of redemption, provoked fear, annoyance and *ressentiment* among disgruntled voters and, the American novelist James Fenimore Cooper said in the 1830s, spread 'intrigue and deception', 'sly cunning and management' and 'appeals to passions and prejudices rather than to reason'.[27]

Let's look at an early case of populism, in Argentina, where in the 1820s the textbook caudillo General Juan Manuel de Rosas (1793–1877) showed how electoral democracy could give birth to a thoroughly modern species of fear-ridden 'democratic caesarism' unknown to the ancients.[28] It's worth remembering that in the age of electoral democracy, Spanish America was no backwater. Between 1810 and 1830, following Napoleon's 1807 invasion of peninsular Spain, every part of its Spanish American empire experimented with the methods of representative self-government. The odyssey turned most of the continent (Brazil remained a slave-owning constitutional monarchy closely tied to Portugal) into the freest place on earth – on paper at least. There was widespread praise for the principles of republican independence, decentralised confederation and check-and-balance federated government. Periodic elections backed by written constitutions, freedom of the press and multi-party systems became fashionable. Several Argentinian provinces daringly set the pace: their suffrage laws, the most advanced in the world, excluded women and indentured labourers with black skin, but otherwise extended the vote to all adult men, regardless of their education or class. 'Every free man,' announced the Law of Buenos Aires in August 1821, 'born in the country or a simple resident, of 20 years of age or above, or before if married, is entitled to vote.'

General Rosas took full advantage of the trend. He touted himself as a brave and fearsome leader, a one-man government who was the saviour of his people and a lovable demagogue. He said he had been saddled with the task of cleansing a 'hell in miniature', a body politic infected with the virus of political anarchy, financial instability and low public morale. On a balmy autumn evening in Palermo, near Buenos Aires, he delivered a passionate speech to his supporters in proto-democratic language under a clump of ombu trees, famous for their wide, creeping roots and hollow trunks. The man who liked to dress in hat and poncho, silver spurs on his heels, whip in hand, ready to mount his horse at any moment, said that his ideal was a form of government defined by 'The autocratic dictators who have been the first servants of the people'.[29]

Rosas set about experimenting with the art of using elections, plebiscites and petitions to outflank his political opponents. The legislature and courts were neutered. Elections were transformed into plebiscites, awash in loud music, oaths of allegiance and fireworks. At every opportunity, Rosas offered perks to his supporters: local justices of the peace, military officers, administrators, journalists at prominent newspapers, ranch owners, wealthy merchants and anybody else willing to become vassals to the great leader. Rosas excelled at encouraging public demonstrations of solidarity. The faithful were instructed to dress in red, the colour of his Federalist forces. Women were urged to carry red flowers, preferably roses, and to wear red ribbons in their hair. The style for men was openly macho: fierce faces; hirsute chests; red caps, bandannas and silk badges calling for death to his enemies.

The man of the People also liked to pose as a man of God. Rosas cosied up to the clergy, many of whom responded by wearing red ribbons, preaching in his favour and organising street processions with portraits of him held aloft, later to be displayed at the rosemary-scented altars of local churches. New infantry and artillery units were meanwhile built up. Nearly half of his annual government budget was eventually devoted to the military, while for reasons of paranoia and megalomania he built a new private police force called the *mazorca*. It functioned as a death squad, carrying out selective assassinations (an estimated 2000 people lost their lives) and sniffing out and hunting down the 'group enemies' of 'The people'. Luckily for the real people of the Argentine provinces, Rosas was toppled by an alliance between his domestic opponents and Brazilian troops, and forced into exile – to Britain, where in recognition of his 'kindness to the British merchants who had traded with his country' he was granted asylum and welcomed with a 21-gun salute. Populism was good for business but bad for democracy.

DEMOCRATIC REVOLUTION

The populism of Rosas showed that electoral democracy was vulnerable to pathologies of its own making, above all endangered by demagoguery the worship of leaders hungry for followers. From the end of the eighteenth century until well into the 1930s, the political matter of who counted as 'The people' triggered other great troubles. Eventually the working classes and women were acknowledged as worthy of the franchise. Some colonial peoples, such as in Senegal, were even blessed with the right to vote. And the formal abolition of slavery happened; in the United States, a bloody civil war marked off the age of electoral democracy from the ancient era of slave-based assembly democracies.

As we have seen, the radical dream of extending and universalising the practice of 'one person, one vote' was born of many different power conflicts, quite a few of them bitterly fought in the name of 'The people' and in opposition to ruling groups, whether princes, bishops and priests, landowners or imperial monarchs. Disputes about who exactly 'The people' were and who was entitled to represent them put every electoral democracy on edge. There were insurrections, boycotts and plenty of state violence. Whether groups, such as the clergy, the propertied classes or people in particular geographic regions, were entitled to privileged representation proved controversial. In Britain, the liberal philosopher and politician John Stuart Mill (1806–1873) championed 'plural voting', with the number of votes enjoyed by each person proportionate to their level of education: an 'ordinary unskilled labourer' would have one vote while a 'graduate of any university, or a person freely elected a member of any learned society' would have at least six.[30]

Strife erupted over the related question of whether and when minorities could legitimately trump the wishes of majorities, to prevent a 'tyranny of the majority' (John Adams), for instance through schemes of proportional representation or by exercising powers of veto and amendment in upper chambers based on different principles of representation. Up until the 1930s, during fits of populism, spiteful politicking and cost-cutting, the governments of Nebraska, Nova Scotia, Prince Edward Island, Manitoba, New Brunswick and Queensland – all states or provinces within a federation – voted to abolish their upper chambers. Federated states more typically preserved their bicameral systems, with upper chambers elected on a different basis of representation, usually territory. Imaginative schemes of 'functional representation' were championed by groups such as the Austro-Marxists and the English guild socialists, who advocated workers' control of industry, joint economic boards and other government plans for enabling workers' representation, of the kind that flourished briefly after World War I in Germany, Czechoslovakia and other central European countries.

The troubles surrounding who was entitled to vote and what representation meant also produced many neologisms, such as 'aristocratic democracy' (that first happened in the Low Countries at the end of the sixteenth century), and new references, beginning in the United States, to 'republican democracy'. Later phrases such as 'social democracy' (coined in Berlin working-class circles around 1840), 'liberal democracy' and 'Christian democracy' – even 'bourgeois democracy', 'workers' democracy' and 'socialist democracy' – also spread.

The new terms expressed the many different kinds of group and class struggles for equal access to government that in the end often resulted, by hook and crook, in victories for the universal franchise in local iterations and institutions. It seemed to millions that the core modern democratic principle of free and fair periodic elections had history on its side. Especially from the second half of the eighteenth century, struggles for representative government and, later, its democratisation, generated great public excitement, pandemonium and hopes for a better future.

With a whiff of empowerment of 'The people' permanently in the air, the final two centuries of the age of electoral democracy unleashed what the nineteenth-century French writer and politician Alexis de Tocqueville (1805–1859) accurately called a 'great democratic revolution' in favour of political and social equality.[31] He noted that electoral democracy promised a dignified way of life based on the equality principle, and predicted that the enslavement of people by 'aristocratic' masters as well as the domination of women by men were among the inequalities that would have trouble surviving the democratic revolution. Excuses and alibis for inequality would sound ever more wooden, and publicly unconvincing.

Tocqueville did worry that the modern democratic revolution might be stifled by an all-powerful paternal state that ushered in a new kind of despotism. He was equally aware that the building of empires – he was among the champions of the French colonisation of Algeria – required clampdowns on electoral democracy, and that colonial rule was therefore vulnerable to democratic resistance by the colonised. His writings display a strong sense that electoral democracy was permanently on trial, but he didn't foresee the organised efforts to roll back the franchise – as in the United States, where African Americans, following the bloody civil war waged in support of their emancipation, found themselves victimised by racist forces bent on narrowing and stealing the right to vote from certain groups, particularly black and poor people.[32] He also underestimated the dangers of populism and, as we're about to see, the challenges posed to electoral democracy by market systems of commodity production and exchange.

And yet Tocqueville was onto something: electoral democracy did indeed help turn the modern world upside-down and

Men casting their votes using ink brushes (*máo bǐ*) during the first Legislative Yuan election in China, held between 21 and 23 January 1948. It was boycotted by the Communist Party and turnout was low, but an estimated 150 million ballots were cast by citizens from the provinces and municipalities, the regions of Tibet and Mongolia, various occupational groups and citizens resident overseas. This was the largest election conducted in the era of electoral democracy and the last contested national election held on mainland soil.

inside-out. It dealt a substantial blow against class hierarchy, male privilege, political bossing and colonial servitude. The modern democratic revolution sent shock waves outwards from the Atlantic region to the whole world. Fuelled by the earliest rowdy struggles and breathtaking acts, such as the artisan uprisings in the Low Countries, the public execution of King Charles I in England and Louis XVI in France, and the slave uprising against French colonial rule in Saint-Domingue (now Haiti), it threw into question all forms of anti-democratic bigotry that treated inequalities among people as 'natural'. Slaves, women and workers won the franchise. At least on paper, and except for indigenous peoples, representation was eventually democratised, to include the bulk of the population. The spirit of electoral democracy took root in the Philippines, where a coalition of middle-class citizens and peasant rebels led by Emilio Aguinaldo proclaimed independence from Spanish imperial rule (the uprising was soon crushed by American annexation and military intervention). Elections also arrived in the Republic of China, where eventually, in 1948, more than 150 million citizens cast their votes in a general election.

WAR AND CAPITALISM

By the early years of the twentieth century, the politics of good government based on votes for all was everywhere on the move. Victory seemed to be around the corner. Italy was sometimes cited as an example of the progress being made: its 1861 general election, dominated by aristocrat powerbrokers, resulted in the unification of the country as the Kingdom of Italy. But change had been fiercely opposed by the Pope; and in any case voting was restricted to literate men over twenty-five who paid taxes. The 1913 general elections remained a man's world, but the right of suffrage was extended to three new categories of men: those who were twenty-one or older and literate; illiterate men who'd reached the age of thirty; and all men who had served in the Italian army or navy. The trend seemed fortuitous. History was on the side of the universal franchise and representative government, or so many observers thought. They were mistaken – deeply mistaken.

Electoral democracy was about to be pushed into swamps teeming with political predators. For a start, no solution was found for the damage caused by imperial rivalries and fierce competition among armed nation-states. From around 370 BCE, during the era of assembly democracy, a remarkable cluster of citizen states in Arcadia, in the Peloponnese, formed themselves into the Arcadian League. Designed to bring peace to a region that had been dominated by Spartan power, the League resembled a simplified version of today's European Union, in that it attempted to fashion a two-tiered confederacy bound by the rules of democratic negotiation and compromise. Run by a regional assembly called the *myrioi*, or 'Ten thousand', it maintained a standing army based at its new capital, Megalopolis. It was the first-ever recorded experiment in cross-border democracy.

Nothing like that happened in the age of electoral democracy. Remarkably, during the 1920s, especially in trade union and social democratic and suffragette circles, there was talk for the first time of 'international democracy'. But in its European heartlands, following a devastating world war, an influenza pandemic and the collapse of every continental empire, the language and practical hopes for cross-border democracy were swept aside. Electoral democracy found itself entrapped in a political inferno in which sovereign territorial states prevailed, locked horns for two decades (1918–1938) and brought on another catastrophic global war. As in the age of assembly democracy, the institutions of self-government were ultimately no match for the death-dealing calamities of war. Electoral democracy buckled, on a global scale.

In his famous Fourteen Points speech in January 1918, outlining a roadmap for ending World War I and fostering collective security, US president Woodrow Wilson (1856–1924) urged leaders and citizens everywhere to support the principle of a 'society of free nations'. There was no mention of electoral democracy, but Wilson clearly had in mind a future in which every state and its people enjoyed self-determination based on law-abiding government and the commitment to free elections, plus freedom of commerce. The desire was to replace war and rumours of war with peaceful cooperation among self-governing states, backed by a 'general association of nations' abiding by 'covenants for the purpose of affording mutual guarantees of political independence and territorial integrity to great and small states alike'. But it proved illusory. Soon there would be just eleven 'free nation' electoral democracies left on our planet.[33]

Two global storms of steel had ruinous effects on the ideals and structures of electoral democracy. The doctrine of self-governing 'sovereign' states protective of their nations, a word often used interchangeably with the phrase 'a people', had promised much. It had offered citizens a sense of purpose and dignity, a feeling of belonging to a bordered territory, of being 'at home' by sharing with others not only the right to vote but also a common understanding of food and songs and jokes and historical memories, even bodily gestures. In practice, the growth of rough-handed states oiled by leaders' fanatical populist appeals to nationhood proved to be divisive, exclusionary and bellicose. Bovine language used by leaders such as Chancellor Otto von Bismarck – 'Germans! Think with your blood!' – helped prepare people for war. In colourful pseudo-democratic language, populist demagogues such as Benito Mussolini then drew the military conclusions. Since 'war is the normal state of the people', he bellowed, 'speeches made to the people are essential to the arousing of enthusiasm for a war'. How best to whet the appetite for battle? Plant 'The national flag' on the 'dunghill' of their popular indignity. Get them to see that there are 'only two fatherlands in the world – that of the exploited and that of the exploiters'. Then, he concluded, the people yearning for self-determination and justice would be willing to march to war for their fatherland, proving that 'fifty thousand rifles' are worth more than 'five million votes'.[34]

The arousal of 'The People' in nation-states armed to the teeth turned out to be Europe's murderous gift to itself, and to the rest of the world. War was the inevitable product of bickering states fuelled by nationalist pretensions. So was civil war, as happened in Ireland, whose partition into two states in 1920 sparked pogroms and gun battles and forced the Catholic minority to live in a Northern Ireland ruled by a British nationalist Protestant majority. Nearly 3000 civilians were killed during the subdivision of the island into two nation-states.

Electoral democracy was equally cursed by another threat for which there was no easy remedy: the challenge of reconciling the democratic vision of equality with the destruction and greed of profit-hungry capitalist economies. We've seen that Greek assembly democracies placed restrictions on commodity production and exchange; when adult male citizens met

Soldiers and fascist paramilitaries raised their black fezzes in honour of Mussolini at a commemoration of the March on Rome in Piazza Venezia on 27 October 1929.

in public, they saw themselves as the higher-order beneficiaries of the necessaries of life produced by women and slaves in the lower sphere of the *oikos*. Politics trumped economics. Assembly democrats didn't believe there was such a thing as an 'economy', whose laws of accumulation had to be respected for the sake of unending economic growth. At various points, the champions of modern electoral democracy also took a stand against the fetishism of economics. In the name of equality, property qualifications for elected representatives were abolished. Electoral democracy helped begin the process of liberating children from the cruelties of starvation, the whip and family bossing and bullying. It made room for independent trade unions, peaceful picketing and political parties committed to ending wage slavery and reckless accumulation.

Factory safety inspectorates and boards of health were established. Local governments were pressured to provide sewers, rubbish removal and clean running water.

The welfare state reforms of the Uruguayan governments led by José Batlle y Ordóñez (1856–1929) were exemplary. They demonstrated for the first time anywhere in Spanish America that it was possible to use the institutions of representative government to create a more egalitarian society – in effect, to produce a type of electoral democracy that rested on more democratic social foundations. Against fierce opposition from hostile employers, Batlle fought tooth and nail for the eight-hour working day, unemployment insurance, night-work restrictions, retirement pensions and enforceable safety standards. The point was to de-commodify everyday life, to weaken the grip of market forces in favour of social equality. Under Batlle's direction, free universal high-school education and women's entry to university were approved. He said repeatedly that education was the right of 'all, without distinction of social class'; at one point, he shocked some citizens by saying that the talented poor should be given the opportunity to become scholars, while the untalented rich should plant potatoes.[35]

These were impressive achievements, but despite them electoral democracy across the world was profoundly damaged by a system of aggressive, profit-driven commodity production and exchange called capitalism. The American political economist Thorstein Veblen (1857–1929) noted how easily electoral democracy could be converted into 'a cloak to cover the nakedness of a government that does business for the kept classes'.[36] Some critics of capitalism emphasised how its promises of 'free labour' were contradicted by the great violence it heaped upon people, whether by freebooters, pirates and slave traders, or by factory industrialists and colonial merchants hungering after wealth. Others noted the way the capitalist mentality corroded the democratic spirit of dignified equality for all people. Capitalism fed and spread greed, an appetite for arbitrary power fuelled by narcissism, vulgar conformity, stupidity and demagoguery.[37]

In a widely read pamphlet circulated shortly after Hitler was appointed Chancellor of Germany, the English public intellectual Harold Laski underscored the practical impossibility of combining capitalism and parliamentary democracy. 'Representative democracy seems to have ended in a cul-de-sac,' he wrote. The ultimate root of the present difficulties, Laski argued, was 'The inability of the principle of equality to find expression in a framework of institutions which deny it the possibility of effective entrance'. That was his way of saying that the chief impediment was an economic system founded on the control rich and powerful individuals, families and corporations had over resources in oil, coal, steel and high finance. Since the 'governing class is not willing to alter the essential characteristics of capitalist society to its disadvantage', the political priority had to be a 'Thoroughgoing institutional adjustment', Laski concluded. Violence was to be avoided. Its use directly threatened the principles and practices of democracy. Instead, the urgent priority was to alter, through trade unions and general elections, the balance of power between the state and the economy by offering 'To the masses the potentiality of capturing the political machinery and using it to redress the inequalities to which the economic régime gives rise'.[38]

Throughout the 1920s and 1930s, similar complaints were issued by millions of citizens and their representatives. They recognised that self-government based on the principle of one person, one vote, wasn't easily reconciled with an economy premised on the concentration of wealth and power in a few hands. There was a background history to the complaints. Yes, there were moments when the ethics and institutions of electoral democracy and capitalism seemed inseparable. The famous formula 'no bourgeois, no democracy' captured the way the spread of capitalism in parts of the world helped erode older forms of unequal dependency of the feudal, monarchic and patriarchal kind.[39] The advance of commodity production and exchange also triggered productive tensions between state power and property-owning and creditor citizens jealous of their public liberties. The principle of 'no taxation without representation' – a child of sixteenth-century cities in the Low Countries – was born of those tensions. The frictions between states and markets also created space for the formation and flourishing of civil societies. The restless dynamism, technical innovation and enhanced productivity of modern capitalism extended material improvement and made possible the rise of a middle class. Capitalism even had the unintended consequence of laying the foundations for the radicalisation of civil society, in the shape of powerful mass movements of workers protected by trades unions, political parties and governments committed to widening the franchise and building welfare-state protections.

Capitalism and electoral democracy seemed to be buddies, but the bitter truth is that the partnership had always been troubled. Electoral democracy found itself threatened by capitalism's rapaciousness, the way it worsened inequality and produced class-structured outcomes, recklessly exploited nature and bred speculative bubbles, whose inevitable bursting generated wild downturns. Throughout the age of electoral democracy, these busts often bred manias and brought fear and misery to people's lives. In the process, they destabilised democratic institutions, forcing them to fall like tender buds in a snap frost – as happened spectacularly, on a global scale, during the 1920s and 1930s.

THE END OF ELECTORAL DEMOCRACY

Besieged by collapsing banks, flights of capital and mass unemployment, electoral democracy in many countries was rocked by great public disturbances, pressures for institutional reform, trumpet calls for revolution against parliamentary government, and state violence. Groups that felt threatened by electoral democracy desperately pushed back. 'The further democratisation advanced,' reports the distinguished historian Jürgen Kocka, 'The more likely it was to find large parts of the bourgeoisie on the side of those who warned against, criticised or opposed further democratisation.'[40] The timing of the bourgeois disaffection with electoral democracy was fateful: it came at the moment when the right to vote for representatives finally came to be seen as a *universal* entitlement. Something had to give. Give it did.

Electoral democracy had appeared to come of age throughout the Atlantic region, including Europe, where between 1919 and 1921 most restrictions on voting were lifted, first for adult men and later – usually much later – for all adult women. But as pressure for the inclusion of women, colonial subjects and the lower classes grew, governments began to be pulled and stretched by multi-party systems that triggered wild swings from one political faction to another. Elections, party competition and power sharing suddenly seemed unfair, ineffective and unresponsive to the needs of millions – not only to the swelling ranks of new voters, but also to landholders and their military allies. Hanging on a hair, governments came and went at an alarming rate; after 1918, there were hardly any European countries blessed by governments that lasted longer than twelve months. Some parliaments suffered a nervous breakdown, made fractious by the multiplication of angry parties and the repeated collapse of executive authority; it was not uncommon to witness chambers ruined by representatives spitting insults, or throwing chairs, as if they were attending a carnival of asses. With civil societies frayed by class, ethnic and national divisions, the resulting social tensions and political conflicts soon took their toll. Parliamentary government imploded. Armed opposition to electoral democracy sprouted devils' horns.

Among the chief foes of democracy during this period were the champions of *purple tyranny*: strong states ruled by monarchs bent on turning back the tide of universal suffrage and parliamentary democracy. Yugoslavia's constitution was rewritten after the 1929 royal coup staged by King

Alexander (who had earlier acceded to the throne because his elder brother was deemed unfit after kicking his servant to death in a fit of rage). The new constitution transferred executive power to the king, who appointed half the upper house of parliament directly, and guaranteed that legislation could become law with the approval of one house alone, so long as it had the king's approval. The new electoral system effectively rolled back the franchise, restoring open balloting in rural constituencies, as public employees were bribed and bullied into voting for the governing party.

Calls for strong leadership and emergency decrees also flourished. The trumpets sounded for *armed dictatorships*, backed by talk of 'The people'. 'I am convinced,' said the Portuguese dictator António Salazar (1889–1970) in 1934, 'That within twenty years, if there is not some retrograde movement in political evolution, there will be no legislative assemblies left in Europe.'[41] He meant it. So did Marshal Józef Piłsudski (1867–1935), former commander-in-chief of the Polish army, who stepped into the political vacuum produced by unstable government, hyperinflation and the assassination of the Polish president, Gabriel Narutowicz (1865–1922). Staging a coup d'état in 1926, Piłsudski rigged elections, gaining 46.8 per cent of the vote in the 1930 elections; arrested and put on trial the main opposition leaders; and, in 1935, imposed a new constitution that legalised dictatorship.

The notable exception to the trend on the European continent was Czechoslovakia. The seventh-largest economy in the world and by far the most durable electoral democracy of middle Europe, it was destroyed from the outside by a third

A mass rally celebration of the 2600th anniversary of Japanese emperors at the Imperial Palace, Tokyo, in November 1940. After the national anthem, music performances, and speeches by prime minister Fumimaro Konoe and Emperor Hirohito, all broadcast live on national radio, the crowd of 50,000 people shouted three times 'Long live His Majesty the Emperor'.

type of anti-democratic politics never before experienced in the history of democracy: *totalitarianism*. It first burst onto the political scene in Russia and Italy, and soon spread to Weimar Germany, whose permanent crisis paved the way for the rise of Hitler; in Japan, there was 'fascism from above', or 'cool fascism', the phrase coined by the journalist Hasegawa Nyozekan (1875–1969). What was so menacing about totalitarianism was its sinister pretence to be a superior form of democracy. Its defenders scorned elections. Hitler harped on about parliamentary democracy as a great threat to natural-born ruling elites. Bespectacled General Tōjō Hideki (1884–1948), wartime leader of Japan's fascist government, banned political parties and, in late April 1942, arranged a 'General Election to Support the Greater East Asia War'. The new totalitarians swore that the totalitarian state was the embodiment of the Sovereign People in the Leader. The 1918 Bolshevik 'Declaration of the Rights of the Working and Exploited People' and the Nazis' pompous talk of a *Volksgemeinschaft*, or 'people's community', expressed the sentiment that totalitarianism was rule of the mobilised masses, for the masses, by the leaders of the masses, backed by the iron fists of uncompromising political power, organised propaganda, terror, concentration camps and the worship of violence.

As if by a conspiracy of devils, the experiences of total war and economic crisis, and the rise of purple tyranny, military dictatorship and totalitarianism together proved that electoral democracy wasn't blessed with inevitability. Its fortunes certainly weren't helped by attacks on its core principles by prominent intellectuals and journalists. Italy's leading liberal, Benedetto Croce (1866–1952), said elections with universal suffrage were recipes for destroying freedom and favouring demagogues and other adventurers. The famous Spanish philosopher José Ortega y Gasset slammed democracy for whipping up spiteful anger and 'morbid' class envy (*ressentiment*) among the plebs. In his *Phantom Public* (1925), America's most distinguished political columnist, Walter Lippmann (1889–1974), caused a minor sensation by suggesting that representative democracy was founded on the bogus myth of 'The sovereign and omnicompetent citizen'. Most voters, he said, had but 'a casual interest in facts'. They were mainly muddled and befuddled creatures, 'as bewildered as a puppy trying to lick three bones at once'.

Similar thinking guided the newfangled business of opinion polling and public relations. The nephew of Sigmund Freud, Edward Louis Bernays (1891–1995), was among its founders. Styling himself a 'public relations counsel', he pushed the frontiers of sampling and public persuasion techniques towards what he called 'The engineering of consent'. He was sure voters were suggestible creatures, driven by libidinal energies in need of sublimation, restraint and ordering. Intelligently crafted publicity blitzes stage-managed by experts and leaders could change beliefs. His contributions to the Committee on Public Information, a Washington-based propaganda unit tasked with convincing the American people that World War I would 'make the world safe for democracy', convinced him of this. Here is Bernays explaining his conviction that electoral democracy had no future:

> The conscious and intelligent manipulation of the organized habits and opinions of the masses is an important element in democratic society. Those who manipulate this unseen mechanism of society constitute an invisible government which is the true ruling power of our country . . . We are governed, our minds are molded, our tastes formed, our ideas suggested, largely by men we have never heard of . . . It is they who pull the wires which control the public mind.[42]

The metaphors were bad news for anyone who still believed that voters in free and fair elections chose their representatives rationally and wisely. Talk of invisible wire-pullers controlling public minds was a frontal assault on the principles of 'government democratical, but representative'. It reminds us that there was no golden age of electoral democracy, simply because – with fewer than a dozen exceptions – almost everywhere in the world, its pure form was stillborn during the first three decades of the twentieth century. Its opponents fought hammer and tongs, and with great success, against its alleged incompetence, its fatal flaws and supposed evil effects. They wanted to prove by their actions that electoral democracy – said by Winston Churchill to be the worst form of government except all those other forms that had hitherto been tried – was mere gibberish. Success came their way. Using radio, newspaper and film propaganda, tanks and fighter planes, poisonous gas, barbed wire and concentration camps, they showed that history could be made to orphan electoral democracy – to kidnap and then kill its soul and substance.

PART THREE

Monitory Democracy

THE STORY OF DEMOCRACY'S PAST so far told in these pages has aimed to mimic the renegade spirit of democracy. It has questioned the reigning narratives fabricated by its enemies, cast doubts on the mental blind spots, tactical errors and prejudices of past democrats, and noted as honestly as possible the uncertainties and great unknowns of democracy's past. Many silenced ancestors of democracy have been granted a voice. Supposing that democracy can only be lived forwards by understanding itself backwards, these pages have made a case for bringing more democracy to the history of democracy.

But the task of discussing the changing contemporary fortunes of democracy – that's formidable. The history under our noses is always the hardest to define and assess. Things are made more challenging by fractious disputes among historians and political thinkers about how to make sense of the changes that are said to have happened or not happened. For some, our generation is a glorious tale of the triumph of 'liberal' democracy. For others, the old spirit of assembly democracy – people deciding things in face-to-face settings – is making a grand return and taking its revenge on the false promises of electoral democracy. Still others say that democracy's fancy goals have been ignominiously cast aside by the predatory forces of state power, populism and capitalism, and that democracy, now facing a global catastrophe for our species as a whole, is suffering creeping irrelevance or terminal decline.[1] These interpretations need to be considered, but they aren't altogether compelling. For one thing can safely be said when looking back on the multitude of happenings since 1945: against tremendous odds, in terrible circumstances, in defiance of economic collapse, dictatorship, totalitarianism and total war, the ideals and institutions of democracy enjoyed a reincarnation. Its 'wild' qualities flourished, pushed along by what came to be called 'people power' – the intrepid resistance and resolve of citizens to put clamps on corrupt, bossy and violent government that had exceeded its limits, abused its authority, failed to deliver on its promises and brought great evils to the world.

This rejuvenation and metamorphosis proved yet again that democratic institutions and ways of life aren't set in stone, and that democracies can democratise by inventing new methods of popular self-government in contexts previously untouched by its spirit. After 1945, the world witnessed the birth of a new species. Sometimes misdescribed as 'liberal democracy', this new type of democracy was neither a Western invention nor synonymous with American-style government. It was something different: a variety of democracy defined by the growth of scores of power-monitoring institutions unknown to earlier democrats. The transformation – the birth of monitory democracy – was astonishing, and it was global. For the first time in history, the lived language of democracy became familiar to most people – even if it often had an American accent. The upshot was that monitory democracy went on trial in all four corners of the world.

The coming of democracy to the southern tip of Africa was a case in point. In mid-February 1990, millions around the world, glued to their televisions, watched Nelson Mandela

(1918–2013) walk free from prison after twenty-seven years. In Cape Town, he was greeted under a molten sun by an estimated crowd of 250,000 people desperately trying to catch a glimpse of their leader. Citizens erupted in song, clenched fists, danced, waved flags; at one point, with megaphone calls to move back inaudible, scores of people took turns to stand or sit on the boot of Mandela's car. So great was the crush that marshals took more than two hours to deliver him to the town hall podium. There, he stood calmly for several minutes, nodding to the assembly gently, before raising his hands for quiet. Punctuated by roars from the crowd, his twenty-minute speech, surely among the greatest in the post-1945 period, announced the beginning of the end of apartheid. 'I have fought against white domination and I have fought against black domination,' he said in a strong, clear voice. 'I have

Nelson Mandela with his then wife, Winnie, arriving at Cape Town City Hall from Victor Verster Prison, greeted by a massive crowd of victorious supporters clamouring to hear their newly freed hero speak his first words.

cherished the ideal of a democratic and free society in which all persons live together in harmony and with equal opportunities. It is an ideal that I hope to live for and to achieve. But if needs be, it is an ideal for which I am prepared to die.'[2]

Almost everywhere it seemed that rulers had lost the plot – and the argument – and were pushed onto the back foot in situations of high drama that doubled as grand media events. In March 1946, the French writer Albert Camus (1913–1960) told a New York audience that the world had been 'ruled by the will to power', torn apart by divisions between masters and slaves and the 'monstrous hypocrisy' of treating human suffering as no longer scandalous. Things had to change. The political task hereon was to 'fight against injustice, against slavery and terror' and to create a world in which people understood that nobody has 'the right to decide that their own truth is good enough to impose on others'. The rhetorical power of Indian prime minister Jawaharlal Nehru's 'Tryst with Destiny' speech – on the eve of the birth of the democratic Republic of India – was later matched by the stirring '*Ich bin ein Berliner*' speech by US president John F. Kennedy, broadcast on radio to millions around the world, during the last week of June 1963. Forgiven by locals for likening himself in bad German to a jam doughnut, Kennedy spoke of the indivisibility of freedom and declared that the world's democrats were eligible for Berlin citizenship. 'Freedom has many difficulties and democracy is not perfect, but we have never had to put a wall up to keep our people in, to prevent them from leaving us,' he said, to wild applause.[3]

In the long wave of democracy that swept through many parts of the globe after 1945, media platforms directed their microphones and cameras at less well-known figures; some of these unknown democrats became global celebrities. A young man, carrying shopping bags, halted a column of Chinese army tanks one day after a massacre in Tiananmen Square. A woman, Aung San Suu Kyi – her name in Burmese means 'a bright collection of strange victories' – faced down a firing squad after troops who'd been ordered to cut short her life suddenly lost their will to pull the trigger.

Miracles didn't always happen. The early decades after 1945 witnessed plenty of setbacks for democracy. This was the case in the oil-rich 'petro-dictatorships' of the Middle East and the former colonies of sub-Saharan Africa, but also in Brazil, where a US-backed military junta ruled with a steel fist for several decades, and the Republic of China, where the results of the January 1948 legislative elections were shredded within months by widespread disorder and the violence of a revolutionary takeover led by the communist forces of Mao Tse-tung (1893–1976). Political scientists pointed out that one-third of the world's thirty-two functioning, multi-party democracies in 1958 had by the mid-1970s lapsed into some form of dictatorship; in 1962, thirteen of the world's governments were products of a coup d'état; by the mid-1970s, the number of military dictatorships had nearly trebled, to thirty-eight.[4]

The military setbacks were frequently vicious – as in Athens in mid-November 1973, when in the name of *dēmokratia* several thousand students barricaded themselves within their campus and used their pirate radio station to broadcast a call for the overthrow of the military government of Colonel Papadopoulos (1919–1999). The dictator replied by despatching a tank to smash through the campus gates; several dozen students and supporters were shot, some by military snipers. At Kent State University on 4 May 1970, the American bombardment of Indochina was brought home against protesting students by masked, heavily armed National Guards, who shot and killed four, wounded nine and forced the rest to crawl to safety through tear gas and puddles of blood and vomit. The massacre was the first time students had been killed in an anti-war gathering in US history. In the former French colony of Algeria, something much worse happened. In late 1991, following the lifting of bans on political parties, the Islamic opposition party Front Islamique du Salut (FIS) won a parliamentary majority. The results were quickly annulled by military intervention. A state of emergency

Wearing red ribbons, wielding a three-fingered victory salute against military slavery, teachers from the Yangon Education University joined the civil disobedience campaign in Myanmar in early February 2021. Following that month's coup d'état, more than 10,000 teachers were suspended and over 700 university and high-school students arrested, many of them tortured.

was declared. FIS and its local and regional council administrations were disbanded. The country was plunged into a decade-long, murderous uncivil war.

Not for the first time in the history of democracy – think of Thailand after the 2014 military coup, or the American colonists' revolution against the redcoats of the British Empire – armed force produced citizen resistance, and some spectacular surprises. There was Costa Rica, which abolished its standing army in 1948; and the political humbling of the Kuomintang (KMT) military government by citizen uprisings in Taiwan.[5] The willingness of military officers to withdraw from the messy business of government was reinforced by the non-violence of their street-level opponents. Given the catastrophes of the twentieth century, democrats everywhere yearned for a world without barbed wire and cattle prods, tanks and tear gas, to live untroubled by the crunch of boots on the streets. 'As a rule,' said the Polish democrat Adam Michnik, 'dictatorships guarantee safe streets and the terror of the doorbell. In democracy the streets may be unsafe after dark, but the most likely visitor in the early hours will be the milkman.'[6] The quip applied to Portugal, where in early 1974 young officers of the Movimento das Forças Armadas felled the dictatorship of Marcello Caetano (1906–1980). Key ministry buildings, postal and telecommunications offices, and broadcasting stations were occupied, along with the country's airports. Huge crowds gathered in the streets of Lisbon to cheer the soldiers on duty. Fresh-cut carnations were slipped into the barrels of their rifles. Caetano surrendered within hours. Following the death of fascist dictator General Franco

On 25 April 1974, mutinous Portuguese troops from the Santarém barracks drove their tanks and other armoured vehicles into central Lisbon and occupied Terreiro do Paço, where nervous citizens offered them pink, red and white carnations. It marked the beginning of a political revolution in favour of what junior officers called 'democratisation, decolonisation and development' (*democratizar, descolonizar e desenvolver*).

in November 1975, the military government of neighbouring Spain suffered the same fate.

Public disgust for military violence surfaced regularly during the following decades. In the Philippines, electoral officers helped trigger the downfall of the military government led by General Ferdinand Marcos (1917–1989) by refusing, in the middle of the night, to carry on counting rigged election ballot papers. In Latin America, Brazil shook off the most violent and criminal dictatorship in its history. The *abertura*, or political opening, re-established freedom of the press along with *habeas corpus*, amnesty for political prisoners, the freedom to form political parties and direct elections for state governors. True to its reputation as the democratic laboratory of Latin America, Uruguay had already set the pace when a decisive majority of citizens (57 per cent) stood against their own military government in a November 1980 plebiscite to decide on a new constitution biased towards the ruling executive power. Since there was still martial law, the victors couldn't take to the streets to celebrate. So they dressed in yellow, the colour of the democratic opposition, and heeded the advice of Montevideo radio-station owner Germán Araújo to spread a 'smile revolution': curls of the lips to demonstrate their magnificent triumph to friends, colleagues and strangers in the streets.

A VELVET REVOLUTION

A sense of urgent joy infused the biggest global victory for the spirit and institutions of democracy after 1945: the citizen uprisings that rocked Estonia, Poland, East Germany and other Central-East European countries and helped trigger the fall of the Soviet empire during the summer and autumn of 1989.

Stunning events that came to be known as the Velvet Revolution gripped Czechoslovakia.[7] The phrase was poached from one of the coolest 1960s New York rock bands, the Velvet Underground, which was ironic considering that the first day of the revolution was littered with ghastly violence.

On the evening of 17 November 1989, a crowd of 15,000 students gathered peacefully outside the Institute of Pathology in Prague to commemorate the death of a student victim of the Nazi occupation fifty years earlier. The commemoration had the ruling Communist Party's blessing; the list of speakers had been compiled by its Communist Youth Union. The mourners were to march to the Slavín tomb in the Prague district of Vyšehrad, where nineteenth-century poet Karel Hynek Mácha (1810–1836) was interred. It was agreed with the authorities that candles would be lit, wreaths and flowers laid, and the national anthem sung, after which the procession would disperse.

It didn't. Thousands of students, feeling their spines straighten, headed spontaneously for Wenceslas Square, singing the national anthem. A flying wedge of grim-faced police wielding truncheons cut into the ranks of the best brains in the country. Shouting and chanting erupted. The sound of boots was temporarily drowned by cries of 'We are unarmed' and 'No violence!' The demonstrators managed to shake off their opponents and march on defiantly, towards the square. Scores of curious bystanders joined in silently, like monks hastening to prayer. Café patrons downed their drinks and joined the throng.

As the demonstration reached the National Theatre, actors and theatre staff joined too. That gave courage to the young demonstrators. They chanted in defiant tones, 'Join us – the nation's helping itself.' Numbers soon mushroomed to more than 50,000; after all the years of isolation, of surveillance and ideological division, it was as if people could not get enough of each other's company.

Around eight p.m., as it entered the avenue Národní Třída, the demonstration was greeted by white-helmeted riot police determined to stop the marchers from reaching the square. Fearing a repeat of a Tiananmen-style massacre, the crowd realised that it was at the mercy of the police. 'We have bare hands,' they cried, but the police, having sealed off all escape routes, attacked the students and dragged hundreds into custody.

And so came the moment when everything changed. 'No violence,' some chanted. Others taunted their captors with 'Freedom!' Still others jangled keys. A handful of women gave flowers to the unsmiling police. Hundreds of candles were lit. 'We have bare hands! No violence! Freedom! Freedom!' the believers in candle-power chanted, yellow light flickering on their faces.

They were soon to get their way. Time was up for communism.

During the night that sparked the Velvet Revolution, Prague protesters responded to police violence at Wenceslas Square by staging a peaceful sit-in, lighting candles, chanting slogans and calling for an end to communist rule.

LIBERAL DEMOCRACY TRIUMPHANT?

The dramatic collapse of the Soviet empire under pressure from 'people power' stirred the imagination of intellectuals, especially in the United States, where rather extravagant 'the world is becoming just like us' interpretations quickly became orthodoxy. A think tank called Freedom House purported to show that in 1900, when monarchies and empires still predominated, there were no electoral democracies with universal suffrage and competitive multi-party elections. There were a few 'restricted democracies' – twenty-five, accounting for just 12.4 per cent of the world's population. By 1950, with the beginnings of decolonisation and the postwar reconstruction of Japan and Europe, there were twenty-two democracies, accounting for 31 per cent of the world's population, and a further twenty-one restricted democracies, covering 11.9 per cent of the world's population. By the end of the century, the report observed, democracy had arrived on the shores of Latin America, post-communist Europe and parts of Africa and Asia. At least on paper, 119 of 192 countries could be described as 'electoral democracies' – 58.2 per cent of the global population. Eighty-five of these – 38 per cent of the world's inhabitants – enjoyed forms of democracy 'respectful of basic human rights and the rule of law'. So the report found that the ideal of 'liberal democracy' was now within practical reach of the whole world. 'In a very real sense,' ran the ebullient conclusion, 'the twentieth century has become the "Democratic Century"', defined by 'the extension of the democratic franchise to all parts of the world and to all major civilizations and religions'.[8]

A similar story was told by 'end of history' man Francis Fukuyama (1952–), who said the collapse of communism proved that 'the class issue has actually been successfully resolved in the West', and the ideals of liberal representative democracy – free and fair elections backed by respect for civil rights and guarantees of private property ownership and free markets – had finally crushed their competitors. Perhaps, speculated Fukuyama, the world now stood at 'the end point of mankind's ideological evolution', with 'Western liberal democracy . . . the final form of human government'.[9]

This was big but biased talk. Its presumption that American-style liberal democracy was the gold standard came as no surprise. It was perhaps to be expected of a global empire whose mainstream intellectuals viewed the world narcissistically, through the narrow lens of its unquestioned self-image. But the certainty was misguided, most obviously because the period since 1945 has witnessed the invention and diffusion of many unusual democratic customs that defied the norms of US liberal democracy. As the world came to be shaped by democracy, we could say, democracy became worldly, more cosmopolitan and less dogmatically liberal.

Consider the thought-provoking but not atypical case of Senegal, the western African country where the importation of elections from Europe showed that democracy could mix with *négritude* (a Pan-African positive sense of blackness) and meld with a predominantly agrarian Muslim society to produce unusual customs that were simply not describable as 'liberal democracy'.[10] Here was a people introduced to Islamic customs from across the Sahara by Berber merchants in the mid-fifteenth century; a territory where electoral politics in limited form dated back to 1848, when (unusually) voting rights were granted by the French colonial authorities to the adult men of the principal urban settlements; a country whose French-speaking elites thought of *démocratie* as a synonym for equality before the law, freedom of association, a free press and the holding of fair and open elections. Under colonialism, voters were only a tiny minority of the population, but the culture of voting and elections gradually spread, culminating in a victory for male and female suffrage in 1956. Following independence in 1960, the government of Léopold Sédar Senghor (1906–2001) did its best to turn the country into a one-party system. Attempts to ban opposition parties and rig elections failed, partly due to strong support for *demokaraasi* among Senegal's Wolof-speaking Muslim majority.

In a remarkable shift of cultural coordinates, some party leaders and journalists, and many citizens, had learned to liken political parties and elections to the sacred place of worship, the mosque. Elections were seen as more than the ousting of a government by ballots, not bullets. They were moments when parties and their leaders resembled muezzins, whose job is to stand atop the minaret to call the faithful – voters – to prayer. Laypeople can become muezzins in Senegalese Islam, so anybody can form and lead a party. Just as at mosque, *demokaraasi* draws on the principle of rotation of muezzins under the supervision of the imam, the one who stands before the assembled faithful to lead them in prayer. Those who head government resemble the imam (the Arabic root of *imām* means 'in front of'); supported by the wider community and supervised

Friday prayers can overflow into the streets in Dakar, Senegal, a country whose citizens, comprising ten distinct ethnic groups, are mostly avowed Muslims.

from a distance by the real holders of power, the religious brotherhoods, leaders are expected to guide others through daily life with the help of parties, on the basis that they have been put in front – chosen – by the wider community.

In practice, the analogy between the mosque and democracy proved challenging. It stirred up public disputes among Senegalese citizens about how imams and politicians are chosen, whether imams have veto rights against elected governments, and how limited-term and lobbied governments can best deal with the realities of poverty, discrimination against women and people of disability, corporate exploitation of natural resources, and tax avoidance. Still, there's no denying that for many Senegalese 'mosque democracy' (as we might call the mutation) was meaningful. For it followed from their way of thinking about *demokaraasi* that it was more than just a mundane method of selecting a government based on community consent; wrapped in sacred language, it was a way of life, a set of beliefs and institutions that bind people together in the presence of the divine. *Demokaraasi* meant sharing resources, mutual recognition, reaching a governing consensus and community solidarity. *Demokaraasi* in this sense knew no distinction between the sacred and the profane. It instead resembled a community of believers bound together by their quest to harmonise their differences through multi-party government and good leadership, under the watchful eye of an exacting God.

THE RISE OF MONITORY DEMOCRACY

Developments in Senegal, South Africa, Brazil and elsewhere showed that in the decades after 1945, democracy was no longer a white-skinned, Western affair – as it had been, say, when Lord James Bryce wrote his classic *Modern Democracies* in 1921, or when a Natal-based historian of democracy spoke of election-based, parliamentary government as 'largely the outcome of the character and historical development of Englishmen', unsuited to 'states where the population does not display the same talents for, or interest in, the management of public affairs'.[11]

Yes, broadly speaking, the many different species of democracies that sprang up on every continent still belonged to the genus called democracy, not just in name, but also in spirit. Political leaders and citizens who thought of themselves as democrats were still bound by respect for non-violent, lawful government based on the consent of 'the people'. They were suspicious of concentrated and unaccountable power; they were committed to the principle that all citizens are equals. But the indigenisation of democracy in environments radically different to the earlier parent electoral democracies of Western Europe, Spanish America and the United States was nevertheless remarkable.

India, soon to become known as the world's 'largest democracy', was no liberal democracy, if that means American-style representative government founded on a large middle class, a free market economy and the spirit of possessive individualism.[12] India's tryst with democracy fundamentally challenged the presumption that economic growth is the core requirement of democracy – that free and fair elections are practical only when a majority of citizens owns or enjoys commodities such as cars, refrigerators and radios. Weighed down by destitution of heart-breaking proportions, millions of poor and illiterate people rejected the prejudice that a country must first be wealthy before it can be democratic. They decided instead that they could become materially stronger *through* democracy. Not only that: the Indian pathway to democracy bearded the woolly predictions of experts who said that French-style secularism, the compulsory retreat of religious myths into the private sphere, was necessary before hard-nosed democracy could happen. The Indian polity contains every major faith known to humanity and is home to hundreds of languages. Social complexity on this scale led Indian democrats to a new justification of democracy. It was no longer a means to protect a homogeneous society of equal individuals. It came to be regarded as the fairest way to enable people of different backgrounds and divergent group identities to live together harmoniously, as equals, without civil war.

India showed that the spirit and substance of democracy were alive globally in local sentiments, languages, institutions and shifting and contested forms of power. After 1945, democracy grew more grounded. But since then something else of historic importance – a transformation less obvious – has been happening: the growth of monitory democracy, a new form of self-government distinctively different from the assembly-based and electoral democracies of the past.

During the 1952 Indian general election, the first held after independence, conservatives claimed that women's involvement in politics threatened ancient caste and gender hierarchies. They had a point: energised by democracy's egalitarianism, women's turnout in elections and contributions to public life have since been rising steadily, often outstripping men's participation, as in the 2015 elections in Bihar, the country's poorest state.

What is monitory democracy? Why the adjective 'monitory' – which first entered English in the mid-fifteenth century (from the Latin *monere*, to warn, to advise) to refer to issuing a warning of an impending danger, or an admonition to check the content or quality of something, or to refrain from a foolish or offensive action? It is a form of democracy defined by the rapid growth of many new kinds of extra-parliamentary, power-scrutinising mechanisms: 'guide dog', 'watchdog' and 'barking dog' institutions. Monitory democracy includes practices such as election monitoring, workplace codetermination and participatory budgeting. It also includes bodies such as future generations commissions, bridge doctors, truth and reconciliation forums and coral-reef monitoring networks. These monitory or public accountability mechanisms are newcomers in the history of democracy. They spring up in many different contexts and are not simply 'Western' inventions.

The rights of workers to elect representatives to their company's governing boards in workplace codetermination schemes (*Mitbestimmung*) first happened in war-torn Germany in the 1940s. Participatory budgeting, in which citizens decide how to spend part of a public budget, is a Brazilian invention. Future generations commissions with statutory power to champion the rights of unborn citizens were born in Wales. Bridge doctors – volunteer teams of university engineering students checking the safety of city bridges – are a South Korean specialty. South Africa made truth and reconciliation forums famous. Coral-reef monitoring networks are a product of global cooperation.

These monitory bodies have taken root everywhere within the local and national fields of government and civil society, as well as in cross-border settings. As a result, the whole architecture of representative government is changing. The grip of elections, political parties and parliaments in shaping citizens' lives and representing their interests is weakening. If electoral democracy rested on the principle of 'one person, one vote, one representative', the guiding ethic of monitory democracy is 'one person, many interests, many voices, multiple votes, multiple representatives'. Under these new conditions, democracy means much more than elections. Within and outside states, independent and toothy watchdog bodies have begun to reshape the landscapes of power. By keeping corporations and elected governments, parties and politicians permanently on their toes, the new watchtowers question abuses of power, force governments and businesses to modify their agendas – and sometimes smother them in public disgrace.

Monitory democracy is the most complex and vibrant form of democracy yet. In the name of 'people', 'the public', 'public accountability' or 'citizens' – the terms are normally used interchangeably – power-challenging and power-tempering institutions are springing up all over the place. Corruption scandals and public outcries against monkey business are becoming the new normal. This does not mean that elections, political parties, legislatures and public assemblies are disappearing or declining in importance, but they are most definitely losing their pole position as hosts and drivers of politics. Democracy is no longer simply a way of handling and taming the power of elected governments, and no longer confined to territorial states. Gone are the days when democracy could be described, and in the next breath attacked, as an abuse of statistics, as 'government by the unrestricted will of the majority'; or, in the oft-cited words of the Moravian-born economist Joseph Schumpeter (1883–1950), the 'institutional arrangement for arriving at political decisions in which individuals acquire the power to decide by means of a competitive struggle for the people's vote'.[13] The age of representative democracy is behind us. Whether we are talking about local, national or supranational government, or the world of non-governmental organisations and networks, those who wield power are now routinely subject to public monitoring and restraint by an assortment of extra-parliamentary bodies.

The advent of monitory democracy challenges earlier, election-centred understandings of democracy. It spells trouble as well for the commonsense view that democracy is essentially a method of controlling governments and taming state power. What's remarkable is how the spirit and power-scrutinising mechanisms of monitory democracy spread 'downwards', into areas of social life previously untouched by democrats. Assembly democracies typically regarded power dynamics within households, and the treatment of women and slaves, as private matters. We saw how the age of representative democracy witnessed resistance to slavery and to the exclusion of women, workers and the colonised from elections. Elected governments intervened in such areas as healthcare and education. One thing that's different about the age of monitory democracy is that it enables, as never before, organised public scrutiny and refusal of arbitrary power in the whole of social life. Matters such as workplace bullying, sexual harassment, racial and gender discrimination, animal abuse, homelessness, disability and data harvesting all become central themes of democratic politics.

Parties, parliaments and elected governments are typically reactive to such issues. Monitory bodies and networks therefore become the true drivers of politics. They help deepen democracy. Its spirit of equality and openness spreads through social life and across state borders. For the first time in the history of democracy, not surprisingly, 'civil society' is a phrase routinely used by democrats at every point on our planet.[14] Monitory democracy springs up wherever there are abuses of power. Uncontested rule in areas ranging from family life to employment is checked – if and when it's checked – not just by elected representatives in government, but also by a host of new institutions that remind millions of citizens of a simple but perennial truth: democracy requires colossal transformations of people's daily lives. Their habits of heart and everyday routines must grow more allergic to abuse of power. To stand against bossing and bullying, people need to nurture the spirit of democracy *within*, as well as to spread it and keep it alive in others. Citizens must be confident that they themselves are the source of power of the institutions that govern their lives; that government and other bodies indeed rest upon the consent of the governed; and that when they withdraw their consent from these institutions and demand alternatives, things can change for the better, even if only in the smallest of ways.

WHY MONITORY DEMOCRACY?

Is this new kind of accountability democracy a sustainable, historically irreversible development? We don't yet know.

A sceptic might ask for more evidence of its novelty, beginning with how it developed. As always in democracy's story, the path of innovation has been circuitous and generalisations are tricky. Monitory democracy has had both its causes and causers; it wasn't hatched from a single cell. It's the product of many forces, including the breakdown of states, citizen disaffection and plain good luck. Plus a vital factor Tocqueville spotted long ago: what could be called the democratic contagion – people's ability to draw the inference that when some of their grievances are remedied, others must also be addressed.[15]

A less obvious but hugely important explanation of the birth of monitory democracy is the role of political catastrophe. In the history of democracy, political breakdown, violence and the pity and suffering of war sometimes yielded more than darkness and despair. The origin of parliaments is an example: against great odds, political crises were midwives of new democratic institutions. That rule applied to the first half of the twentieth century, the most murderous in recorded human history. An economic depression plus two global wars punctuated by terrible cruelties against whole populations shattered old structures of security, sparked aggression and elbowing for power, and unleashed angry popular energies that fed major upheavals – including attacks on electoral democracy in the shape of Bolshevism and Stalinism in Russia, fascism in Italy, Nazism in Germany and military imperialism in Japan. These regimes denounced electoral democracy as parliamentary dithering, liberal perplexity, bourgeois hypocrisy and military cowardice. In consequence, near the mid-point of the twentieth century, democracy was on its knees – spiritless, paralysed, doomed. By 1941, when President Roosevelt called for 'shielding the great flame of democracy from the blackout of barbarism' while untold numbers of villains had drawn the contrary conclusion that dictatorship and totalitarianism were the future, fewer than a dozen electoral democracies remained.[16]

Then something extraordinary happened. The carnage produced by war, dictatorship and totalitarianism prompted thinkers and writers from across the political spectrum to bring about a shift in the definition and ethical justification of democracy. They helped trigger a moment of what physicists and astronomers call 'dark energy': in defiance of the gravity of contemporary events, the universe of meaning of democracy underwent a dramatic expansion. The German writer Thomas Mann (1875–1955) gave voice to the trend in noting the need for 'democracy's deep and forceful recollection of itself, the renewal of its spiritual and moral self-consciousness'. Others expressed shock and dismay at the way the electoral democracies of the 1920s and 1930s had facilitated the rise of demagogues (German philosopher Theodor Adorno dubbed them 'glorified barkers'). These populists were skilled at calling on 'the people' to mount the stage of history – only to muzzle, maim and murder in the people's name, so destroying the freedom and political equality for which electoral democracy had avowedly stood. There was general agreement that the recent catastrophes proved the naivete of the formula that people should obey their governments because their rulers protect their lives and possessions. This pact was no longer workable; worse, it was politically dangerous. The problem was no longer 'mob rule' by ignorant, unkempt commoners, as critics of democracy had insisted from Plato and Thucydides until well into the nineteenth century. Totalitarianism proved that mob rule had its true source in thuggish leaders skilled in the art of manipulating and seducing 'the people'. Ruling through brute force and cunning was now the fundamental political problem.

And so it was during the 1940s that a fresh historical form of democracy was imagined.[17] Its distinctive spirit and new institutions were marked by a militant commitment to casting out the devils of arbitrary, publicly unaccountable power. The Irish man of letters C.S. Lewis (1898–1963) captured the point: 'A great deal of democratic enthusiasm descends from the ideas of people . . . who believed in a democracy because they thought mankind so wise and good that everyone deserved a share in the government. The danger of defending democracy on those grounds is that they're not true.' The 'real reason for democracy' is that 'no man can be trusted with unchecked power over his fellows'.

The Chinese writer Lin Yutang (1895–1976), whose *My Country* and *My People* enjoyed a wide readership during this period, put the same point in pithier terms. Politicians aren't 'benevolent rulers' who 'love the people as their own sons'; far better to treat them as 'potential prison-inmates' and 'devise ways and means to prevent these potential convicts from robbing the people and selling the country'. Democracy hereon had to suppose that people were 'more like potential crooks than honest gentlefolk', and that since they can't be expected always to be good, 'ways must be found of making it impossible for them to be bad'.[18]

From left to right on the political spectrum, a global assortment of writers, theologians, scientists and scholars voiced fears that parliamentary democracy's narrow escape from the clutches of economic collapse, war, dictatorship and totalitarianism might just be a temporary reprieve. Deeply troubled, they called for new remedies for the maladies of electoral democracy, beginning with the abandonment of sentimental optimism about 'popular sovereignty'. There was widespread rejection of pseudo-democratic, fascist talk of 'the will of the people'. Joseph Schumpeter, who served as Austria's first finance minister and made and lost a fortune as an investment banker before becoming a Harvard professor, warned that 'groups with an ax to grind' have a nasty habit of 'staging and managing political shows' bent on manufacturing 'the will of the people'. The French Catholic philosopher and early champion of human rights Jacques Maritain (1882–1973) insisted that 'the people are not God, the people do not have infallible reason and virtues without flaw'. The BBC radio lectures by J.B. Priestley (1894–1984) – broadcast on Sunday evenings through 1940 and again in 1941, drawing peak audiences that rivalled Churchill's – repeated the point by asking, 'Who are the people?' His answer, with Hitler on his mind:

> The people are real human beings. If you prick them, they bleed. They have fathers, mothers, sisters, brothers, sweethearts, wives and children. They swing between fear and hope. They have strange dreams. They hunger for happiness. They all have names and faces. They are not some cross-section of abstract stuff.[19]

The 1940s rebels knew too much. Their sadness and alarm were too deep for tears. They had witnessed how electoral democracy had been a weak opponent and a willing accomplice of totalitarian destruction. They were defiant, sure that the greed for unlimited power and murderous spell cast by the new totalitarians had to be resisted. That is why they reasoned that a radical alteration of the language of democracy was needed. Democracy had to be talked about differently – and practised in novel ways. In these despairing times, the poetry mattered: without new words, new meanings, no new democracy could emerge. These rebels were certain that the fetish of elections and majority rule was dangerous folly. Its grip on the democratic imagination had to be broken. Democracy was too precious to be left to politicians and governments; the old belief that elections are its heart and soul was a great mistake. Badly needed was a new commitment to democracy understood as the protection of citizens from cowing and coercing, the celebration of diversity and the reduction of social inequality using methods in addition to free and fair elections.

The rebels didn't quite put things this way, but in effect they called for a second round of democratisation of the 'sovereign people' principle of electoral democracy. We've seen already that the reimagining of electoral democracy kickstarted the work of humbling the metaphysical principle of 'the people'. The whole idea of electoral democracy underscored the importance of political leadership. It also cleared the way for the admission, absent in the ancient Athenian understanding, that any given democracy must provide room for legitimate differences of public opinion and divisions of material interest. The rebels took things further. The task was as much theoretical as practical: to ensure that democracy could function as a weapon against all forms of abusive power, including evils perpetrated by elections conducted in the name of a fictional 'sovereign people'.

This much was agreed. But opinions here divided, for instance over the merits and perils of private property and free-market competition against concentrated state power. The drafter of the Indian constitution, B.R. Ambedkar (1891–1956), was among those who cautioned that unbridled capitalism would plague democracy with a 'life of contradictions' generated by the conflict between the struggle for good government based on political equality and a society ruined by huge social and material inequalities. Many commentators recommended the building of public-spirited welfare-state institutions in support of the right to a decent education and universal healthcare. Others went further by championing workers' right to vote for representatives on the board of directors of their company – the extension of the principle of elected representation into the heartlands of the market, as later happened in Germany, Denmark, France, Sweden and other countries.

Disagreements aside, most of the rebels supported a form of democracy whose spirit and institutions were infused with a robust commitment to dealing with the devils of unaccountable power. The American theologian Reinhold Niebuhr (1892–1971), who later won prominent admirers, including Martin Luther King Jr (1929–1968), delivered one of the weightiest cases for renewing and transforming democracy along these lines. 'The perils of uncontrolled power are perennial reminders of the virtues of a democratic society,' he wrote in *The Children of Light and the Children of Darkness* (1945). 'But modern democracy requires a more realistic philosophical and religious basis, not only in order to anticipate and understand the perils to which it is exposed, but also to give it a more persuasive justification.' He concluded with words that became famous: 'Man's capacity for justice makes democracy possible; but man's inclination to injustice makes democracy necessary.'[20] The remark implied a new understanding of democracy as the continuous public scrutiny, tempering and control of power according to standards 'deeper' and more universal than the old reigning principles of periodic elections, majority rule and popular sovereignty.

Capturing the new spirit, political thinker Hannah Arendt (1906–1975) called for active confrontation with the demons of arbitrary power. 'The problem of evil,' she wrote in 1945, 'will be the fundamental question of post-war intellectual life in Europe.' In fact, the hurts and pains caused by unchecked power were a *global* problem. In perhaps the boldest move of the period, some thinkers proposed ditching the reigning presumption that the 'natural' home of democracy was the sovereign territorial state, or what the distinguished French jurist René Cassin (1887–1976) – disabled Jewish World War I veteran, De Gaulle's chief legal adviser, co-author of the Universal Declaration of Human Rights and condemned to death by the fascist Vichy government – dubbed the Leviathan State. So they pleaded for extending the democratic principle of equality of power across territorial borders. 'The history of the past twenty years,' the German scholar Carl Friedrich (1901–1984) wrote, 'has shown beyond a shadow of a doubt that constitutional democracy cannot function effectively on a national plane.' Thomas Mann similarly repudiated state-centric definitions of democracy. Multilateral institutions could help protect vulnerable minorities and liberate citizens from narrow-minded nationalism and abuses of power by states and businesses. 'We must reach higher and envisage the whole,' he said. 'We must define democracy as that form of government and of society which is inspired above every other with the feeling and consciousness of the dignity of man.'[21]

COMMUNICATIVE ABUNDANCE

If democracy was now to be understood as the ongoing struggle for self-government backed by new forms of public accountability, the practical challenge was to find in these grimly tempestuous times of the 1940s methods of placing constraints on dangerous concentrations of power. Although greater citizen participation in public affairs was widely recommended, especially at the city and workplace levels, scrapping representative politics and returning to Greek-style assembly democracy was unpopular; it was seen as incapable of meeting the large-scale challenges of the dark times. Far bolder and more forward-looking measures were needed. Countries such as the Federal Republic of Germany (1949) and India (1950) responded by adopting written constitutions designed to prevent abuses of power by imposing duties on elected governments to respect the fundamental rights of their citizens. The worldwide growth of monitory organisations, networks and campaigns committed to the protection of human rights was another innovation.

The crowning achievement of the decade was the Universal Declaration of Human Rights. Drafted in 1947–1948 in response to genocide in the aftermath of global war, the declaration – the most translated document ever, today available in 500 languages – proclaimed a series of rights to be enjoyed by everyone, 'without distinction of any kind, such as race, colour, sex, language, religion, political or other opinion, national or social origin, property, birth or other status'. Its preamble spoke of 'the inherent dignity' and 'the equal and inalienable rights of all members of the human family'. The declaration in effect solved a basic problem that had dogged assembly and electoral democracy: who decides who 'the people' are? The redefinition of democracy as the global protection and nurturing of human rights gave an answer: every human being is entitled to exercise their right to have rights, including the right to prevent arbitrary exercises of power through independent public monitoring and free association with others. In practice, that meant no elected government was entitled to ride roughshod over any individual or group anywhere. Torture, the abuse of women, cruelty to children, rigged elections, religious discrimination and media censorship were not permissible – even when carried out in the name of 'democracy' and a 'sovereign people'.

The authors of the Declaration of Human Rights included René Cassin (second from left); Chinese playwright, literary critic and diplomat Peng-chun Chang (third from left); chair of the drafting commission Eleanor Roosevelt (centre); and Lebanese Thomist thinker of Greek Orthodox convictions Charles Malik (third from right), who presented the final draft to the United Nations General Assembly on 10 December 1948.

The new way of thinking about democracy proved to be the candle in the gloom bred by the death of forty-five million people, terrible physical destruction and spiritual misery, and the mounting post-war tensions bound up with such political troubles as the bloody partition of Pakistan and India, the Berlin blockade and the architectural cleansing and expulsion of hundreds of thousands of Palestinians from their homeland by the British-backed state of Israel. Impressive was how the reimagining of democracy enabled the design of scores of power-tempering institutions that had never existed before in the history of democracy. The age of monitory democracy has seen the application of the rules of representation, democratic accountability and public participation to an ever-wider range of settings, including citizen assemblies, teach-ins, climate strikes, anti-corruption commissions and constitutional safaris (famously used by the drafters of the new South African constitution to examine best practice elsewhere). And let's not forget Indonesian local religious courts, Indian public interest litigation, consumer testing agencies, medical councils, war crimes tribunals, democracy cafés, peer review panels, investigative journalism and web platforms dedicated to tracking and stopping the abuse of power.

The wide range of innovations turned out to be good for the democratic principle that who gets how much, when and how should depend on an active citizenry as well as the public scrutiny and restraint of power, and not just on bland talk of 'the right to vote' or democracy limited to elections. Monitory democracy in this sense still today feeds upon the spirit of resistance to arbitrary power dating back to the 1940s. But most of the recent democratic innovations have come to depend heavily for their vitality on an equally significant driver: the digital communications revolution, which has been reshaping institutions and the daily lives of people globally during the past half-century.

Too little attention is paid to the way that all historical forms of democracy are grounded within and shaped by communication media, so let's for a moment think of things in this way: assembly-based democracy belonged to an era dominated by the spoken word, backed up by laws written on papyrus and stone, and by messages dispatched by foot, donkey or horse. Electoral democracy sprang up in the era of print culture – the book, pamphlet and newspaper, and telegraphed and railway-delivered messages – and fell into crisis during the advent of early mass broadcasting media, especially radio, cinema and (in its infancy) television. By contrast, monitory democracy has come to be tied to multimedia-saturated societies – whose structures of power are continuously tracked and resisted by citizens and representatives acting within digital media ecosystems. This world of communicative abundance is structured by linked media devices that integrate text, sound and images, and enable communication to take place through multiple user points, within modular global networks accessible to many hundreds of millions of people scattered across the globe. Monitory democracy and computerised media networks are conjoined twins. If the new galaxy of communicative abundance suddenly imploded, monitory democracy would probably not survive.

We know about the organised manipulation of information by hidden algorithms, corporate data harvesting, political gaslighting, state surveillance and other decadent trends, yet equally striking is the way the decadence breeds stiff public resistance. Communicative abundance feeds the restless spirit of monitory democracy.[22] It never pauses. Compared with the era of electoral democracy, when print culture and limited-spectrum audio-visual media were aligned with and could be controlled by political parties and governments, the age of monitory democracy witnesses constant spats about power, to the point where it seems as if no organisation or leader or area within government and civil society is immune from political trouble. Every nook and cranny of power becomes the potential target of 'publicity' and 'public exposure'. Birth and death, diet and health are stripped of their certainties. Police violence and abuses of power against religious, racial and sexual-preference minorities are no longer considered 'normal', or excused. The public handling of a global pestilence and its implications for wealth distribution, jobs and wellbeing are widely seen as political matters. In the era of communicative abundance, no hidden topic is protected unconditionally from media coverage, and from possible politicisation; the more 'private' it is, the more 'publicity' it often gets. Nothing is sacrosanct – not even the efforts of those who try to protect or rebuild what they claim to be sacrosanct. Past generations would find the whole process astonishing in its scale and democratic intensity. With the click of a camera or the flick of a switch, hidden worlds can be made public: everything from the bedroom to the boardroom, the bureaucracy to the battlefield. Citizens and investigative journalists using multiple media platforms keep alive the utopian ideals of shedding light on power, freedom of information and greater transparency in government and business. Little wonder that public objections to wrongdoing and corruption are common in the era of monitory democracy. There seems to be no end of scandals; and there are even times when scandals, like earthquakes, unsettle whole political orders.

DEMOCRACY'S GREENING

In the age of monitory democracy, some scandals become legendary – such as the whopping lies about weapons of mass destruction spun by the defenders of the disastrous US-led military invasion of Iraq in the 2000s. In a time when every field of power is potentially the target of 'publicity' and 'public exposure', new types of public dissent also happen – strikingly, in exchanges between humans and non-human environments.

For the first time in democracy's history, monitory institutions conduct campaigns to block wanton environmental destruction and issue public warnings about an uninhabitable future Earth. Most obviously, green political parties help lead the charge – the first in the world were the United Tasmania Group in Australia and the Values Party in New Zealand in the early 1970s. Independent statutory bodies such as the UK's Climate Change Committee are briefed to keep governments on track to achieve net zero carbon emissions. Global bio-agreements, such as the Convention on Biological Diversity, the Aarhus Convention, and the 2015 Paris Agreement, call upon states to guarantee their citizens information about and participation in environmental decision-making. Environmental impact hearings and citizen science projects – such as the UK's Open Air Laboratories (OPAL) project, which encourages people to act as stewards of their local environments – proliferate. Climate strikes and multimedia civic insurgencies like Extinction Rebellion multiply. Large-scale Earthwatch summits, bio-regional assemblies, green think tanks and academies, and conventions to protect regional marine environments sit alongside local initiatives, such as building butterfly and bee 'bridges' in urban spaces to protect endangered species from traffic. For the first time, there are victories for the legal redefinition of lands deemed to enjoy 'all the rights, powers, duties and liabilities of a legal person', as in New Zealand's (Aotearoa's) *Te Urewera Act 2014*.

Also for the first time there are constitutional clauses designed to protect the biosphere, which radically alter the meaning of citizenship in a democratic political order. Chapter 2, Article 6 of Mongolia's constitution expressly states

Extinction Rebellion, a non-violent civil disobedience initiative that aims to prompt government and business action on climate, dug up the lawn around Isaac Newton's apple tree at Trinity College, Cambridge, in February 2020. The excavation – a calculated mimicry of the college's continuing investment in coal and gas mining – generated international media coverage and prompted the college to disinvest $20 million in fossil fuels and commit to net zero emissions by 2050.

that citizens must enjoy rights to a 'healthy and safe environment, and to be protected against environmental pollution and ecological imbalance'. Article 70A of Slovenia's stipulates that 'everyone has the right to drinkable water', while Article 5 of the Kingdom of Bhutan's specifies that every citizen must contribute to the conservation of Bhutan's rich biodiversity and to the prevention of ecological degradation, including visual, noise and physical pollution, by supporting and adopting environment-friendly practices and policies. There are also trend-setting land management and environmental stewardship schemes backed by indigenous self-government, for instance in the Haida Gwaii (Islands of the People) in the north-east Pacific and Uluru-Kata Tjuta National Park in Central Australia.

All these experiments have great significance for the way we think about democracy. They are infused with a strong democratic sense of the dynamic and fragile complexity of our world. They raise awareness of the interconnectivity of all living and nonliving elements and foster deep respect for the nonhuman and its legitimate right to be represented in human affairs. There's more: these watchdog platforms craft new ways of shaming and chastening human predation. They suppose that, in order to secure the clean air, water and food humans need to thrive, people must become guardians of the places where they live. They urge people to see the wondrous in the common, and to value the commons. They probe the reasons why people don't act in order to get them to act. They insist that some things are not for sale and highlight the costs of public ignorance of climate change, species destruction and 'development'. These platforms call upon humans to swap their innocent attachments to talk of 'the economy' and ideologies of 'GDP growth', 'progress' and 'modernisation' with a more prudent sense of deep time that highlights the fragile complexity of our biosphere and its multiple rhythms.

These viridescent platforms help complicate and enrich everyday understandings of democracy. They force a redefinition of democracy, ridding it of its anthropocentrism by asking: why suppose 'the people' are the pinnacle of creation, lords and ladies of the universe, the rightful masters and possessors of 'nature' because they are the ultimate source of sovereign power and authority on Earth? These watchdog platforms grant a political voice to the biosphere. They reconnect the political and natural worlds in what the French anthropologist Bruno Latour (1947–) aptly calls 'parliaments of things'. 'Law should not be centered around Men, but around Life', the argument runs.[23] This is more than urging humans to reimagine themselves as humble beings whose fate is deeply entangled with the ecosystems in which they dwell. Democracy is redefined to mean a way of life that renders power publicly accountable – through elected and unelected representative institutions in which humans and their biosphere are given equal footing.

HARD TIMES

The new environmental guardians specialise in issuing warnings that unless we humans have the courage to change our ways, things may turn out badly – so badly that the ideals and institutions of monitory democracy will perish, along with millions of biomes and living species that might also include the species questionably known as *Homo sapiens*. We've seen how democracies in times past were bedevilled by losses of self-confidence and bouts of self-destructiveness. During the late fourth century BCE, when Athens faced invasion by Alexander the Great, records show that its citizens grew so despondent that more than once the whole assembly slumped into silence when confronted by bad news. During the 1920s and 1930s, many electoral democracies lost their bearings, surrendered to their enemies or bumbled into committing democide. The spreading sense among millions of people that democracy is now endangered is on a par with these previous periods of despondency. But it is different. These warnings – which date back to the 1940s, when fears of global nuclear annihilation first surfaced – are without precedent. It is not only that the new sentinels are alerting publics to the growing frequency of environmental catastrophes and their cascading effects. Never before has it been said by so many that democracy must be set aside, at least temporarily; that there is no time for prevarication and piecemeal reforms when our planet is facing a civilisational crisis that requires drastic action to save our species.

The alarm about the global fate of democracy is compounded by a cluster of other anxieties. High on today's list of complaints is the hollowing out of representative government by the forces of centralised state power – the drift towards what Thomas Jefferson called 'elective despotism'. A prominent historian of democracy, Pierre Rosanvallon (1948–), claims the centre of political gravity in contemporary democracies has shifted from political parties, elections and parliaments towards strong-armed executive rule. The legislative branch of government is now subordinate to government by the few. The 'age of presidentialism' is upon us. It breeds citizen dissatisfaction and loud complaints about 'leaders making decisions without consultation, failing to take responsibility for their actions, lying with impunity, living in a bubble'.[24]

The change resembles a slow-motion coup d'état – helped along by tactics such as gag orders, leak investigations, hidden payments, the appointment of acting heads of government departments without the approval of the legislature, as used during the presidency of Donald J. Trump. Compounded by rulers' willingness to mobilise the machinery of government to enforce extended lockdowns during COVID-19 in countries such as Germany and South Africa, there are signs that elective despotism is triggering not only citizen disaffection and grumbling about politicians, but also morbid complaints against 'democracy' itself. More than a few say things are going worse than anybody expected. Many think democracy is fucked.

A 27-country survey conducted in 2019 found that 51 per cent of interviewees were 'not satisfied with the way democracy is working'. Researchers at the Economist Intelligence Unit documented a steady ten-year waning confidence in democracy between 2007 and 2017, and a marked rise in citizens' concerns about transparency, accountability and corruption. A prominent Scandinavian democracy monitoring body has noted that 'the aspects of democracy that make elections truly meaningful are in decline. Media autonomy, freedom of expression and alternative sources of information, and the rule of law, have undergone the greatest declines among democracy metrics in recent years.' An American think tank was gloomier. 'Democracy is in crisis,' it concluded. 'The values it embodies – particularly the right to choose leaders in free and fair elections, freedom of the press, and the rule of law – are under assault and in retreat globally.'

Measured in terms of the future resilience of monitory democracy, perhaps the most worrying finding is that young people are almost everywhere the least satisfied with democracy and – as if they have seen through the official pageantry and pretence and wooden reassurances of their elders – more disaffected than previous generations at the same age.[25]

There are unwelcome findings in India, which is fast becoming the world's largest failing democracy. Support for democracy among its people dropped from 70 per cent to 63 per cent between 2005 and 2017. The proportion of citizens 'satisfied' with democracy plunged from 79 per cent to 55 per cent; dissatisfaction was lower still among those with tertiary educations (47 per cent). More than half of respondents in the 2010–2014 period said they'd back 'a governing system in which a strong leader can make decisions without interference from parliament or the courts', up from 43 per cent in 1999–2004. Respect for the armed forces runs unusually high; together with Vietnam, South Africa and Indonesia, India is one of only four countries where a majority of citizens (53 per cent) say they would support military rule. In its *Democracy Report 2020*, Sweden's V-Dem Institute noted that India 'has almost lost its status as a democracy' and ranked the country below Sierra Leone, Guatemala and Hungary. In its follow-up 2021 report, V-DEM described India as an 'electoral autocracy'. [26]

There's also discouraging news from Latin America, where reportedly less than a quarter (24 per cent) of citizens are happy with the way democracy is working in their countries, the lowest figure since survey polling began. Many complain about social injustices linked to poverty. More than 40 per cent of Argentina's forty-five million people – and nearly 60 per cent of its children – live in shantytown poverty. After 2000, when the shift to multi-party democracy in Mexico began, the number of people officially living beneath the poverty line increased to more than 50 per cent of the population. Fed by a reserve army of the poor, mafia violence has grown by alarming proportions. Scores of elected city mayors have been assassinated, several hundred journalists murdered or disappeared, and more than a quarter of a million citizens have been robbed of their lives.

Many observers point out that much citizen disaffection is traceable to the widening gaps between rich and poor, which make a mockery of the principle of democratic equality. Symptomatic is the way that during the first year of a global pandemic, the total wealth of billionaires in countries such as India, Sweden, France and the United States more than doubled. Almost every democracy is feeling the pinch of the old rule that capitalism and democracy are ultimately incompatible, and it seems we're again living through a period when the egalitarian spirit of democratic self-government is reduced to a mantra that functions as 'a cloak to cover the nakedness of a government that does business for the kept classes'.[27] Daily life is being scarred by the growth of plutocracy, meritocratic elites and the emergence of a substantial 'precariat' of under- and part-time employed people in gig-economy jobs that pay poorly and have no union protection or long-term security.

Little despot, big despot: a brewing bromance between Hungary's president Viktor Orbán and Russia's Vladimir Putin at a Budapest press conference announcing new deals for purchasing Russian nuclear energy technology and gas supplies from energy giant Gazprom in February 2015.

Leading political thinkers are pointing out that the damage done to democratic institutions by 'corporate power, the corruption of the political and representative processes by the lobbying industry . . . and the degradation of political dialogues promoted by the media' are 'the basics of the system, not excrescences upon it'. They warn of the birth of a 'managed democracy' and 'inverted totalitarianism' in which private corporations seize control of government with the help of commercial media that demobilises and shepherds the citizenry.[28] Corporate power's colonisation of democratic institutions has led some historians to turn the 'third wave of democracy' and 'triumph of liberal democracy' stories on their head, to say that ever since the 1970s, democracy, at least in the West, has been disfigured by the 'triumvirate power of business, banking and political leaders'. State policies of 'saving capitalism' have weakened trade unions, promoted deregulation of public services and spread the culture of consumption fuelled by private credit and the belief in the 'sanctity of the unobliged individual'.[29]

THE NEW DESPOTISM

That's not all. The mood of despondency about the socially and politically damaging effects of environmental despoliation, concentrated state power, and threats posed by financial turbo-capitalism is compounded by rising awareness that monitory democracies are facing a new global competitor: despotic regimes that in Turkey, Russia, Hungary, the United Arab Emirates, Iran and China have a top-down political architecture and capacity to win the loyalty of their subjects using methods unlike anything known to the earlier modern world.

Like vultures pecking at rotting flesh, the critics of monitory democracy are enjoying once-in-a-lifetime feasts of cynicism and rejection of power-sharing democracy. Chinese critics are especially scathing in their attacks on American-style liberal democracy. Scholar Su Changhe believes a key priority is to 'pull apart the language of Western democracy', for 'to have a truly free spirit and an independent national character, [China] must first take the idea of democracy promoted by a minority of Western countries and demote it from universal to local'. The People's Republic mustn't fall into the 'democracy trap' that produces 'social divisions, ethnic antagonism, political strife, endless political instability and weak and feeble governments', he writes. Chinese journalist Thomas Hon Wing Polin adds that 'Western-style liberal democracy is but one form of democracy. It neither puts the people in charge, nor their interests uppermost. It is at the bottom an oligarchy that serves the interests of a tiny minority at the expense of the vast majority.'

China's best-known sci-fi writer, Liu Cixin, is even blunter. 'If China were to transform into a democracy, it would be hell on earth,' he told *The New Yorker* in 2019, a provocation that reappears in a scene towards the end of his bestselling trilogy *Remembrance of Earth's Past.* It describes the disasters triggered by the invasion of an alien species that quarantines most of Earth's population onto the Australian continent. 'The society of resettled populations transformed in profound ways,' Liu writes. 'People realised that, on this crowded, hungry continent, democracy was more terrifying than despotism. Everyone yearned for order and a strong government.'[30]

Order and strong government sanctioned by 'the people' is exactly what's offered by the self-confident rulers of a new crop of despotisms that are a global alternative to power-sharing monitory democracy. These rulers are strengthened by their subjects' belief that the thing called Western democracy is falling apart. Hence their temptation to confront monitory democracies, to challenge them on a global scale, just as dictatorships, monarchies and totalitarian regimes did a century ago when encircling electoral democracies. The new despotisms aren't old-fashioned tyrannies or autocracies or military dictatorships. And they mustn't be confused with twentieth-century fascism or totalitarianism.

Despotism is rather a new type of strong-armed state led by tough-minded rulers skilled in the arts of manipulating and meddling with people's lives, marshalling their support and winning their conformity. Despotisms craft top-to-bottom relations of dependency oiled by wealth, money, law, elections and much media talk of defending 'the people' and 'the nation' (the phrases are often interchangeable in local languages) against 'domestic subversives' and 'foreign enemies'. Despotisms are top-down pyramids of power, but it's a mistake to suppose they are based simply on repression and raw force. They strive to practise nimble governance. They do more than repeat and repeat again the mantra of 'popular sovereignty'. Their leaders harness public opinion polling agencies, think tanks, election campaigns, happiness forums, policy feedback groups, online hearings and other early warning detectors of dissent. The rulers of the new despotisms are deception and seduction perfectionists. They are masters of phantom democracy. They do all they can to camouflage the violence they use on those who refuse to conform. Using a combination of slick means, including calibrated coercion masked by balaclavas, disappearances and back-room torture, they manage to win the loyalty of sections of the middle classes, workers and the poor. They labour to nurture their willing subjects' docility. Voluntary servitude is their thing. And they travel in packs. The new despotisms, led by a newly confident China, are skilled at navigating multilateral institutions to win business partners and do military deals well beyond the borders of the states they rule.

While Erdoğan, Putin and other new despots claim to practise their own forms of 'democracy' grounded in the authority of 'the people', they have no love of monitory democracy. Their true passion is power, exercised arbitrarily over others. They can be ruthless and vengeful in its pursuit, using military means, as in Syria, Kazakhstan and Ukraine. Yet they are not blindly reckless. They normally pay meticulous attention to details, cleverly interfere with people's lives, stand over them, issue targeted threats and bully dissenters into submission. The public support these rulers enjoy is thus surprising, especially when it's considered that despotisms are state capitalist regimes dominated by poligarchs – rich government and businesspeople who concentrate staggering amounts of wealth in their own hands, and within the family dynasties they control and protect.

Democracies such as Britain, Spain and the most powerful of them all, the United States, are also warped and weighed down by massive inequalities of opportunity and wealth. Other ingredients of despotic power are alive and well *inside* monitory democracies, too. Think of the way a new kind of 'surveillance capitalism', run by giant state-backed data-harvesting corporations such as Amazon and Google, is colonising, manipulating and reshaping the personal lives of many millions of people

'So you want democracy?' the policeman asks the begging dogs, in a satirical cartoon circulated widely on Chinese microblogging site Weibo in 2016. The harmony produced by strong, well-armed government is contrasted with the false promises, disorder and violence of Western-style democracy.

for the sake of profit and power, without their consent and regardless of election outcomes. Or how elected populist governments in Brazil, India, Poland and Mexico are potentially midwives of despotism. Trump's four-year presidency set the pace: nourished by disaffected citizens and corporate donations, his government spread disinformation, undermined the rule of law, picked fights with enemies, discredited expertise and investigative journalism ('fake news') and generally accelerated the drift towards strong-armed rule. During elections, he promised redemption for all. In practice, in the name of a fictional 'people' and helped by dark money and tighter links between government and business, his presidency favoured top-down rule by the few of the many.

In these and other ways, democracies serve as the incubators of despotism. When it's also considered that democracies and despotisms are entangled in cross-border chains of shadowy power, and cooperate in transport infrastructure projects, banking and arms deals, it should be clear that the principles and practices of constitutional power-sharing democracies, as we have known them since the 1940s, are threatened not only by outside political rivals. Hungary, Kazakhstan and Turkey – to name just several cases – show that a transition from a power-sharing democracy to despotism can happen rapidly, in not much more than a decade.[31] These cases serve as warnings that monitory democracy can be snuffed out by stealth, bit by bit, using governing methods that bear a strong resemblance to those found in China, Russia, Iran, Saudi Arabia and elsewhere. These new despotisms should wake up democrats everywhere, reminding them that they are living through times in which the writing is on democracy's wall.

WHY DEMOCRACY?

And so, through the thickening fog and dooming gloom, we must ask some basic questions: just as electoral democrats succumbed and collaborated with their opponents during the 1920s and 1930s, why shouldn't today's democrats just give in to the despotism alternative and bid adieu to the ideals and institutions of power-sharing, monitory democracy? Doesn't realism dictate the need to accept the urgings of Putin, Erdoğan and other despots, to concede that the time has come to prepare the last rites for the 'Western' shambles called monitory democracy? To see that the new world order emerging from the collapse of the Soviet Union, current European stagnation, disorder in the Arab world, the decline of the American empire, the return of a belligerent Russia and a self-confidently ambitious China favours top-down despotism, not democracy? In short, why be on the wrong side of history? Why cling to that old-hat thing called democracy?

Why indeed should different peoples with diverse interests at different points on our planet favour monitory democracy as a way of life? Why must they commit to greater public accountability, the humbling of the powerful and the equalisation of life chances for all? Could democracy instead be a fake global norm, a pseudo-universal ideal that jostles for attention, dazzles with its promises and, for a time, seduces people into believing that it is a weapon of the weak against the strong – when in reality it is just organised bribery of the poor by the rich, an ignorant belief in collective wisdom, an accomplice of human crimes against nature, a pretentious little value peddled by second-rate shopkeepers with second-rate minds (as the nineteenth-century German anti-philosopher Friedrich Nietzsche thought)?[32] Said differently: is monitory democracy really to be valued in Cape Town and Caracas as much as in Chennai, Canberra, Copenhagen and Chongqing?

In tackling these ethical questions, retrieving and breathing life into past justifications of democracy isn't an option because – here comes a surprise! – the history of democracy is littered with dogmatic, strangely anti-democratic and self-contradictory justifications as to why democracy is a universal norm. Take a few examples from the age of electoral democracy. The nineteenth-century Christian view, expressed in American publisher Nahum Capen's (1804–1886) attempt to write the first full-length history of democracy, was that democracy is desirable because it draws inspiration and truth from the Gospels – that's bad news for Muslims, Hindus, Confucians and others.[33] Early modern champions of national sovereignty insisted that each Nation (they liked the upper case) was entitled to govern itself, and that struggles for national self-determination had History on their side – in practice, the doctrine proved often to be murderous, such as for Irish Catholics, condemned to be underdogs in a dominant nation-state; or for Palestinians and Kurds, who were stateless; or for Romany, Sámi, Inuit and other indigenous peoples who were deemed unfit for nationhood. And an influential tract called *Government* (1820), written for an encyclopaedia by the Scottish preacher and civil servant James Mill (1773–1836), explained that representative democracy was the protector of private property and possessive individualism and the guarantor of the utilitarian principle that 'if the end of Government be to produce the greatest happiness of the greatest number, that end cannot be attained by making the greatest number slaves'.[34]

Philosophically speaking, the trouble with these old justifications isn't only that they are in contradiction. They suffer from single-mindedness. They presume their justification of democracy is universally applicable because it rests on a timeless first principle that requires democrats, as well as all their opponents, to bow down in its presence. That philosophical conceit of course rubs against the self-questioning and levelling spirit of democracy. Talk of God, Nation, History and Private Property is not just doctrinaire metaphysics. Its pontifical quality contradicts the whole idea of monitory democracy as the defender of an open diversity of ways of life freed from the bossy dictates of the high-and-mighty.

The resort to justifying democracy by looking at its positive practical consequences is equally unconvincing. For instance, democracy isn't always a promoter of peace – the empires of Athens and present-day Israel and the United States show exactly the opposite. It's not the universal precondition of market-generated wealth or sustained or sustainable 'economic growth' – ask the Chinese or Vietnamese governments, or green activists, about that claim. And to say that democracy fosters 'human development more fully than any feasible alternative' – as did American political thinker Robert Dahl (1915–2014) – raises difficult questions about the meaning of the terms 'human' and 'development', and ignores non-human dynamics.

And so the search begins for fresh ethical justifications of democracy that rely on more rigorously humble ways of thinking, without clinging to platitudes such as 'democracy is good because it lets people decide how they want to live', or by cynically embracing a 'nothing is true and anything goes' relativism that inevitably sides with the enemies of democracy who say it is mere tripe and twaddle.

Is there a way to escape the double trap of dogmatism and relativism? There is. What's needed are lateral ways of reimagining democracy as our universal ideal because it is the guardian of plurality – the protector of different ways of living freed from the dictates of arrogant, violent and predatory power.

Thinking of democracy as the guardian of open-minded diversity and the champion of publicly accountable power makes the ethic of democracy more capacious, more universally tolerant of different and conflicting definitions of democracy, and more capable of respecting the fragile complexity of our human and non-human worlds. It parts company with the lurid philosophical search for timeless first principles, but it doesn't accept that thinking about democracy must hereon travel light, following the path of pragmatic calculation.[35] In these embattled times, thinking about the merits of monitory democracy requires more thought, not less reflection.

Of course, in the villages and cities of Nigeria, Indonesia, Chile, Brazil and other countries, the word 'democracy' is typically not treated as a philosophical matter. When it is prized, it is for much less esoteric reasons, to do with uncorrupted, elected governments providing clean running water, electricity, vaccinations and decent schools and hospitals. It's also true that elsewhere 'democracy' serves as a code of commonsense belief. 'Have faith in democracy,' said outgoing US president Barack Obama. 'It's not always pretty, I know. I've been living it. But it's how, bit by bit, generation by generation, we have made progress.'[36] Considered as a way of life, monitory democracy draws strength from these and other sentiments in its favour. But they aren't enough. For when the going gets rough and times are troubling, a compelling argument for democracy really counts. It can make a difference to public opinion and the power dynamics within any given context. It can persuade people to hold fast to their commitment to democracy, or to change their minds in its favour, to see and feel things differently – above all to recognise the need to rein in any form of power that harms their lives by bringing them hardship, sorrow and indignity.

The suggestion that the problem of abusive power should be central to how we think about democracy is a vital clue why it can be considered indispensable everywhere. If democracy is understood as an unending process of humbling unconstrained power, then we must abandon all earlier efforts to link it to arrogant first principles. 'Democracy is not figurable,' writes the French scholar Jean-Luc Nancy (1940–2021).[37] Like water, it has no fixed form or substance. Not only does it vary through time and space, as we have seen, but its defiance of fixed ways of living and refusal of all forms of top-down power masquerading as 'normal' or 'natural' are compelling. Democracy has a punk quality. It is anarchic, permanently unsatisfied with the way things are. The actions unleashed by its spirit and institutions create space for unexpected beginnings. Always on the side of the targets and victims of predatory power, democracy doubts orthodoxies, loosens fixed boundaries, widens horizons and pushes towards the unknown.

Thinking of democracy as a shape-shifting way of protecting humans and their biosphere against the corrupting effects of unaccountable power reveals its radical potential: the defiant insistence that people's lives are never fixed, that all things, human and non-human, are built on the shifting sands of space-time, and that no person or group, no matter how much power they hold, can be trusted permanently, in any context, to govern the lives of others. We could say, thinking back to the age of the first popular assemblies, that democracy is a means of damage prevention. It's an early warning system, a way of enabling citizens, and whole organisations and networks, to sound the alarm whenever they suspect that others are about to cause them harm, or when calamities are already bearing down on their heads. Nietzsche famously complained that democracy stands for the disbelief in rule by elites and strongmen. It does, and for good reason. Democracy brings things back to earth. It serves as a 'reality check' on unrestrained power. It is a potent means of ensuring that those in charge of organisations don't stray into cuckoo land, wander into territory where misadventures of power are concealed by fine words, lies, bullshit and silence.

When thought of in this way, the early warning principle of democracy counts as a global good. Mention of democracy no longer courts humdrum fantasies of bringing peace, economic growth or humanity to people, or indulges university-seminar illusions of citizens inspired by rational deliberation to join hands in harmonious agreement. It requires giving up dogmatic attachments to a first principle, be it Truth or Happiness or Human Rights or Nation or Market or the Sovereign People. It refuses to indulge worn-out put-downs of democracy as 'government by orgy, almost by orgasm' (as the Baltimore writer H.L. Mencken said in his attack on the 'primitive appetites and emotions' of 'the lower orders of men' in his 1927 *Notes on Democracy*). It urges critics who today trash it as a synonym for spineless liberal muddle or Western arrogance to think again about the perils of uncontrolled power. Profoundly suspicious of power exercised arbitrarily, a champion of the weak and the wise against the strong and the foolish, the early warning principle of democracy applies equally to the criss-crossing worlds of everyday life and big business, local and national governments and international organisations. It's constantly on watch for all forms of arbitrary power, wherever they take root. It warns that catastrophes usually result from group think, wilful blindness and other pathologies of unchecked power. It is therefore just as applicable to poorly designed and badly run mega-projects in China's Belt and Road Initiative, multi-billion-dollar tar-sand extraction projects in Canada and the corporate extinction of forests in Brazil as it is to the secretive 'modernisation' of military forces or risky credit and banking sector ventures in London, Amsterdam, Shanghai and New York.

Gripped by a strong sense of reality as fluid and alterable, democracy is a fair-minded defender of openness, a friend of perplexity when in the company of those who exercise power with cocksure certainty. Nothing about human behaviour comes as a surprise: it sees that humans are capable of the best, and perpetrators of the worst. For that reason, democracy stands against every form of hubris. It considers concentrated power blind and therefore hazardous; it reckons that humans are not to be entrusted with unchecked rule over their fellows, or the biomes in which they dwell. It upends the old complaint that democracy resembles a ship of fools, or a rollicking circus run by monkeys. Democracy stands against stupidity and dissembling; it is opposed to silent arrogance and has no truck with bossing, bullying and violence. Its role as an early warning system makes it attuned to conundrums and alive to difficulties. It warns citizens and their representatives about the possible dangers of unknown consequences of consequences of consequences. It is serious about the calamities of our times, and it tracks the calamities to come.

When reimagined in terms of the precautionary principle, monitory democracy, the most power-sensitive form of self-government in the history of democracy, is clearly the best weapon so far invented for guarding against the 'illusions of certainty'[38] and for breaking up monopolies of unaccountable power, wherever and however they operate. Seeing democracy in this way doesn't suppose, philosophically speaking, that it is a True and Right golden standard. Just the reverse: the ethic of monitory democracy is the precondition of breaking the grip of moral swagger. The ethic of democracy is aware of its own and others' limits, aware that democracy is not 'natural' and aware that it has no meta-historical guarantees. It doesn't indulge arrogant idiots. It refuses the humiliation and indignity of people. Power on stilts is not its thing.

Democracy doubts talk of good kings and queens, benevolent dictators and smart despots. In an age when millions of people sense they have lost control over how political decisions are made, democracy questions the arrogant and takes the side of the powerless against those who abuse their power. It well understands that the defence of social and political pluralism can be pushed to the point where diversity destroys the conditions that make pluralism possible in the first place. It knows that the powerless can turn against power sharing. Populism shows that the ship of democracy can indeed be sunk by its mutinous sailors. With the practical help of a plethora of power-humbling mechanisms, democracy nevertheless supposes that a more equal world of well-being, openness and diversity is possible. It champions these ideals not because all women and men are 'naturally' equal, or because they are anointed by God or the deities or 'modernisation' or History. Instead, democracy shows us that no man or woman is perfect enough to rule unaccountably over their fellows, or the fragile lands and seas in which they dwell.

Is that not wisdom of global value?

Notes

INTRODUCTION

1. Lin Yutang, *My Country and My People*, William Heinemann, London and Toronto, 1948 (first published 1936), p. 198.

PART I: ASSEMBLY DEMOCRACY

1. A translation of the text appears in W.G. Lambert, *Babylonian Wisdom Literature*, Oxford, London, 1960, pp. 112–15.
2. See Francis Joannès, '*Haradum et le pays de Suhum*', *Archéologie* 205, September 1985, p. 58: 'Concerning the silver, which Habasanu during his tenure as mayor had made the town pay, the entire town assembled and spoke in these terms to Habasanu: "Of the silver which you made us pay, a great amount has stayed in your house, as well as the sheep which we gave on top as voluntary gifts."'
3. For further details of these republics (called *gana dhina*) – whose assemblies appear to have been dominated by warrior aristocrats (*kshatriya*) but also included ritual specialists (*brahmana*) and merchants (*vaisya*), although not labourers (*shudra*) – see Jonathan Mark Kenoyer, 'Early City-States in South Asia: Comparing the Harappan Phase and Early Historic Period', in Deborah L. Nichols and Thomas H. Charlton (eds), *The Archaeology of City-States: Cross-Cultural Approaches*, Smithsonian Institution Press, Washington and London, 1997, pp. 51–70; Ananat S. Altekar, *State and Government in Ancient India*, Motilal Banarsidass, Delhi, 1958; Jagdish Sharma, *Republics in Ancient India: c. 1500 BC–500 BC*, E.J. Brill, Leiden, 1968; and Romila Thapar, 'States and Cities of the Indo-Gangetic Plain c. 600–300 BC', in *Early India: From the Origins to AD 1300*, University of California Press, Berkeley and Los Angeles, 2002, pp. 137–73.
4. The account of Wen-Amon is translated in James Henry Breasted, *Ancient Records of Egypt: Historical Documents from the Earliest Times to the Persian Conquest*, University of Chicago Press, Chicago, 1906, volume 4, §§ 557 ff.

5. Aristotle, *Politics*, 1304a 31–3; ibid. 1303a 22–4 and 1311a 39.
6. Plato, *Republic*, 557 BCE and 492 BCE.
7. Produced in 424 BCE, the scathing satire features a chorus of young aristocrats (the knights) who side with the sausage seller, Agoracritus, in his efforts to control Demos by outmanoeuvring his current overseer, a slave called the Paphlagonian. The two coarse rivals for power over Demos resort to flattery and Greek gifts: in order better to control him, they praise Demos as Tyrant and Sole Ruler of the Earth, and tempt him with everything from freshly trapped rabbits and cheap fish to pillows to soften the stone seats at the Pnyx. Demos appears pleased by the trickery: he is depicted, through most of the play, as a conceited rogue whose foolishness is compounded by his insistence that he knows precisely what is going on.
8. Jean-Jacques Rousseau, *Du contrat social ou principes du droit politique*, Larousse, Paris, 1973 (first published 1762), book 3, chapter 15, p. 168.
9. Plato, *Statesman* 291 D 1–29 A 4.
10. Thucydides, *History of the Peloponnesian War*, 2.37–45; see Kurt A. Raaflaub, 'Democracy, Power, Imperialism' in J. Peter Euben et al. (eds), *Athenian Political Thought and the Reconstruction of American Democracy*, Cornell University Press, Ithaca and London, 1994, pp. 103–46.

PART II: ELECTORAL DEMOCRACY

1. Thomas Jefferson to Isaac H. Tiffany, 26 August 1816, retrieved from The Thomas Jefferson Papers at the Library of Congress, http://hdl.loc.gov/loc.mss/mtj.mtjbib022558
2. David Runciman, 'The Paradox of Political Representation', *The Journal of Political Philosophy*, volume 15, no. 1, 2007, pp. 111–12.
3. Baron de Montesquieu, *The Spirit of the Laws*, Hafner Press, New York and London, 1949 (first published 1748), book 2, chapter 2 ('Of the Republican Government, and the Laws in Relation to Democracy'), p. 9.
4. René-Louis de Voyer d'Argenson, *Considérations sur le gouvernement ancien et présent de la France*, Chez Marc Michel Rey, Amsterdam, 1764, p. 8.
5. James Madison, 'The Utility of the Union as a Safeguard Against Domestic Faction and Insurrection (Continued)', *Daily Advertiser*, 22 November 1787: 'The two great points of difference between a democracy and a republic are: first, the delegation of the government, in the latter, to a small number of citizens elected by the rest; secondly, the greater number of citizens, and greater sphere of country, over which the latter may be extended.'

6. Alexander Hamilton to Gouverneur Morris, 19 May 1777, in Harold C. Syrett and Jacob E. Cooke (eds.), *The Papers of Alexander Hamilton*, Columbia University Press, New York, 1961, volume 1, pp. 254–56.
7. From a speech by James Wilson to the Federal Convention, 6 June 1787, in Max Farrand (ed.), *The Records of the Federal Convention of 1787*, Yale University Press, New Haven and London, 1937, volume 1, chapter 13, document 18, pp. 132–33.
8. Henry Brougham, *Political Philosophy*, H.G. Bohn, London, 1849, part 3, chapter 6, p. 33.
9. Thomas Jefferson, 'Thomas Jefferson to Benjamin Rush [17 August 1811]', in William B. Parker and Jonas Viles (ed.), *Letters and Addresses of Thomas Jefferson*, Unit Book Publishing, New York, 1905, p. 204.
10. Thomas Paine, *Rights of Man*, J.S. Jordan, London, 1971, part 1, pp. 272–74.
11. ibid.
12. A.F. Pollard, *The Evolution of Parliament*, Longmans, Green & Company, London and New York, 1920, p. 3; an identical claim is made by Alan F. Hattersley, *A Short History of Democracy*, Cambridge University Press, Cambridge, 1930, pp. 78–79.
13. Friedrich Nietzsche, *Beyond Good and Evil: Prelude to a Philosophy of the Future* (trans. W. Kaufmann), Vintage, New York, 1966, p. 202.
14. Alexander Henderson, *The Bishops' Doom: A Sermon Preached before the General Assembly Which Sat at Glasgow Anno. 1638, On Occasion of Pronouncing the Sentence of the Greater Excommunication against Eight of the Bishops, and Deposing or Suspending the Other Six*, John Gray and Gavin Alston, Edinburgh, 1792, pp. 17–18.
15. Walter Thomas Mills, *Democracy or Despotism*, University of California, Berkeley, 1916, p. 61.
16. Francisco I. Madero, *La sucesión presidencial en 1910: El Partido Nacional Democrático*, Colección Reforma-Revolución, Mexico, 1908, pp. 179–85, 230–41.
17. Gyula (Julius) Schvarcz, *Die Demokratie von Athen*, E. Avenarius, Leipzig, 1901, volume 1, pp. 29–69.
18. Cited in Terry Golway, *Machine Made: Tammany Hall and the Creation of Modern American Politics*, Liveright, New York, 2014, p. 106.
19. Alexander Keyssar, *The Right to Vote: The Contested History of Democracy in the United States*, Basic Books, New York, 2001, p. 98.

20. Paul Groussac's remarks are found in his *Del Plata al Niágara*, Administracion de la Biblioteca, Buenos Aires, 1897); Bolívar's confession is cited in Enrique Krauze, *Redeeemers: Ideas and Power in Latin America*, New York, 2011, p. 342.
21. Conservative Party founding statement in Ludolf Parisius, *Deutschlands politische Parteien und das Ministerium Bismarcks*, J. Guttentag, Berlin, 1878, pp. 219–20; Henry Sumner Maine, *Popular Government*, John Murray, London, 1886, p. 36, who added that democracy resembled 'a mutinous crew, feasting on a ship's provisions, gorging themselves on the meat and intoxicating themselves with the liquors, but refusing to navigate the vessel to port' (pp. 45–46).
22. From a letter to Captain Mercer, 26 February 1790, in *Correspondence of the Right Honourable Edmund Burke: Between the Year 1744, and the Period of his Decease, in 1797*, F. & J. Rivington, London, 1844, p. 147.
23. Catherine Cleverdon, *The Woman Suffrage Movement in Canada*, Toronto University Press, Toronto, 1950, p. 215.
24. François Guizot, *Histoire des origines du gouvernement représentatif, 1821–1822*, 1822, Didier, Paris, translated as *The History of the Origins of Representative Government in Europe*, Henry G. Bohn, London, 1861, part 1, lecture 1, p. 12.
25. Charles F. Adams (ed.), *The Works of John Adams*, Little, Brown & Co., Boston, 1856, volume 6, p. 469.
26. Benjamin Franklin, 'Madison Debates', 26 July 1787, retrieved from Lillian Goldman Law Library, Yale Law School, https://avalon.law.yale.edu/18th_century/debates_726.asp
27. James Fenimore Cooper, *The American Democrat: Or, Hints on the Social and Civic Relations of the United States of America*, C.K. McHary, Cooperstown, 1838, pp. 122–23.
28. The phrase 'democratic caesarism' was the title of a most interesting, still untranslated work by the Venezuelan diplomat, former customs officer, scholar, journalist, publisher and director of the national archives, Laureano Vallenilla Lanz, *Cesarismo democrático. Estudios sobre las bases sociológicas de la constitución efectiva de Venezuela*, Empresa El Cojo, Caracas, 1919.
29. From the interview with Rosas by Vicente G. and Ernesto Quesada (Southampton 1873), in Arturo Enrique Sampay, *Las ideas políticas de Juan Manuel de Rosas*, Icon Juárez, Buenos Aires, 1972, pp. 215, 218–19; the Palermo speech is described in the correspondence of Enrique Lafuente to Félix Frías, 18 April 1839, in Gregorio F. Rodríguez (ed.), *Contribución histórica y documental*, Casa Jacobo Peuser, Buenos Aires, 1921–22, volume 2, pp. 468–69.

30. John Stuart Mill, 'Thoughts on Parliamentary Reform' (1859), in J.M. Robson (ed.), *The Collected Works of John Stuart Mill, Volume XIX: Essays on Politics and Society*, University of Toronto Press, Toronto, 1977, pp. 322–25.
31. Alexis de Tocqueville, *Democracy in America* (ed. J.P. Mayer), Doubleday, Garden City, 1969, volume 1, p. 12.
32. Alexander Keyssar, *The Right to Vote: The Contested History of Democracy in the United States*, Basic Books, New York, 2000.
33. Twelve months into World War II, the surviving electoral democracies included Australia, Canada, Chile, Costa Rica, New Zealand, Sweden, Switzerland, the United Kingdom, the United States and Uruguay. Despite its use of an electoral college to choose a president under high-security, wartime conditions, Finland might also be included in the band of survivors.
34. The quotations are from 'Duce (1922–42)', *TIME*, 2 August 1943; Emil Ludwig, *Talks with Mussolini* (trans. Eden and Cedar Paul), Allen & Unwin, London, 1932; Stephen J. Lee, *Aspects of European History, 1789–1980*, Taylor & Francis, London, 1988, p. 191; and Christopher Hibbert, *Benito Mussolini: The Rise and Fall of Il Duce*, Penguin Books, Harmondsworth, 1965, p. 40.
35. José Batlle y Ordóñez, '*Instrucción Para Todos*', *El Día*, 4 December 1914.
36. Thorstein Veblen, *The Vested Interests and the Common Man*, B.W. Huebsch, New York, 1946 (first published 1919), p. 125.
37. Max Scheler, *Trois essais sur l'esprit du capitalisme. Sauvés par le travail?*, Éditions Nouvelles Cécile Defaut, Nantes, 2016.
38. Harold J. Laski, *Democracy at the Cross-Roads*, National Council of Labour, London, 1934.
39. Barrington Moore, Jr., *Social Origins of Dictatorship and Democracy*, Beacon Press, Boston, 1966, p. 418.
40. Jürgen Kocka, *Capitalism Is Not Democratic and Democracy Not Capitalistic*, Firenze University Press, Firenze, 2015, p. 24.
41. Cited in F.C. Egerton, *Salazar, Rebuilder of Portugal*, Hodder & Stoughton, London, 1943, pp. 224–27.
42. Walter Lippmann, *The Phantom Public*, Routledge, New Brunswick and London, 1993 (first published 1925), pp. 15, 28; Edward Bernays, *Propaganda*, H. Liveright, New York, 1928, pp. 9–10.

Notes

PART III: MONITORY DEMOCRACY

1. Examples of these various interpretations include Francis Fukuyama, *The End of History and the Last Man*, Free Press, New York, 1992; Wolfgang Streeck, *How Will Capitalism End? Essays on a Failing System*, Bloomsbury, London, 2017; David Stasavage, *The Decline and Rise of Democracy: A Global History from Antiquity to Today*, Princeton University Press, Princeton, 2020; and Nadia Urbinati and Arturo Zampaglione, *The Antiegalitarian Mutation: The Failure of Institutional Politics in Liberal Democracies*, Columbia University Press, New York, 2013.
2. Kader Asmal et al. (eds), *Nelson Mandela in His Own Words: From Freedom to the Future*, Little, Brown, London, 2003, p.62; the speech is available at https://www.youtube.com/watch?v=-Qj4e_q7_z4
3. The full audio text of the speech delivered in West Berlin on 26 June 1963 can be found at www.americanrhetoric.com/speeches/jfkichbineinberliner.html
4. Sidney Verba, 'Problems of Democracy in the Developing Countries', Harvard–MIT Joint Seminar on Political Development, remarks, 6 October 1976; Samuel E. Finer, *The Man on Horseback: The Role of the Military in Politics*, Penguin, Harmondsworth, 1976, p. 223.
5. John Keane, 'Asia's Orphan: Democracy in Taiwan, 1895–2000', in *Power and Humility: The Future of Monitory Democracy*, Cambridge University Press: Cambridge and New York, 2018, pp. 61–74.
6. Cited in John Keane, *Violence and Democracy*, Cambridge University Press, Cambridge and New York, 2004, p. 1.
7. A full account of the Prague events is to be found in John Keane, *Václav Havel: A Political Tragedy in Six Acts*, Bloomsbury, London and New York, 1999.
8. See Freedom House, 'Democracy's Century: A Survey of Global Political Change in the 20th Century', New York, 1999.
9. See Francis Fukuyama, 'The End of History?', *The National Interest*, Summer 1989; and my interview with him, 'On the Road to Utopia?', *The Independent*, 19 June 1999.
10. The classic study is Frederic Charles Schaffer, *Democracy in Translation: Understanding Politics in an Unfamiliar Culture*, Cornell University Press, Ithaca, 2000; see also Sheldon Gellar, *Democracy in Senegal: Tocquevillian Analytics in Africa*, Palgrave Macmillan, New York, 2005, pp. 156–71.
11. Alan F. Hattersley, *A Short History of Democracy*, p. 237.
12. Debasish Roy Chowdhury and John Keane, 'Tryst with Democracy', in *To Kill A Democracy: India's Passage to Despotism*, Oxford University Press, Oxford and New York, 2021, pp. 3–37.

13. Friedrich von Hayek, *Law, Legislation and Liberty, Volume 3: The Political Order of a Free People*, University of Chicago Press, London and Henley, 1979: 'I must frankly admit that *if* democracy is taken to mean government by the unrestricted will of the majority I am not a democrat, and even regard such government as pernicious and in the long run unworkable' (p. 39); Joseph Schumpeter, *Capitalism, Socialism, and Democracy*, Harper & Brothers, New York and London, 1942, p. 269.
14. John Keane, 'Hopes for Civil Society', *Global Perspectives*, volume 1, no. 1, August 2020, pp. 1–11.
15. Alexis de Tocqueville, *The Old Régime and the French Revolution* (trans. Stuart Gilbert), Garden City, 1955 (first published 1856), part 3, chapter 4, p. 177: 'Patiently endured so long as it seemed beyond redress, a grievance comes to appear intolerable once the possibility of removing it crosses men's minds. For the mere fact that certain abuses have been remedied draws attention to others and they now appear more galling; people may suffer less, but their sensibility is exacerbated.'
16. President Franklin D. Roosevelt, Address to the White House Correspondents' Association, Washington, 15 March 1941.
17. The radical rethinking of the global future of democracy during the 1940s is discussed at length in John Keane, *Power and Humility*.
18. C.S. Lewis, 'Equality' (1943), in Walter Hooper (ed.), *Present Concerns: Essays by C.S. Lewis*, Harcourt Brace Jovanovich, New York, 1986, p. 17, paragraph 1; Lin Yutang, *My Country and My People*, pp. 277–78.
19. J.B. Priestley, *Out of the People*, Collins, London, 1941, pp. 16–17, 111; Jacques Maritain, 'Christianity and Democracy', typewritten manuscript prepared as an address at the annual meeting of the American Political Science Association, New York, 29 December 1949; Joseph Schumpeter, *Capitalism, Socialism and Democracy*, p. 263.
20. Reinhold Niebuhr, *The Children of Light and the Children of Darkness: A Vindication of Democracy and a Critique of its Traditional Defenders*, Nisbet, London, 1945, p. vi.
21. Hannah Arendt, 'Nightmare and Flight' (1945), in *Essays in Understanding 1930–1954*, Harcourt Brace & Company, New York, 1994, p. 134; Carl J. Friedrich, *Constitutional Government and Democracy*, Little, Brown, Boston, 1941, p. 34; and Thomas Mann, *The Coming Victory of Democracy*, Yale University Press, London, 1943, p. 22.
22. John Keane, *Democracy and Media Decadence*, Cambridge University Press, Cambridge and New York, 2013; see also Ronald J. Deibert, *Reset: Reclaiming the Internet for Civil Society*, House of Anansi, Toronto, 2020.

23. Bruno Latour, 'From Realpolitik to Dingpolitik or How to Make Things Public', in Bruno Latour and Peter Weibel (eds), *Making Things Public: Atmospheres of Democracy*, MIT Press, Cambridge, 2005, pp. 14–41; Bruno Latour, *We Have Never Been Modern*, Cambridge, 1993; and 'The Parliament of Things', https://theparliamentofthings.org/

24. Pierre Rosanvallon, *Good Government: Democracy Beyond Elections* (trans. Malcolm DeBevoise), Harvard University Press, Cambridge, 2018, pp. 2–19. The interpretation is insightful but hampered by lack of clarity about the timing of the transition (variously described as 'over the last two centuries' and 'some thirty years') and excessive reliance on the case of France. The proposed democratic reforms for a 'permanent democracy' equipped with robust 'mechanisms of vigilance and oversight' and 'accountability' look much like the monitory democracy born of the 1940s.

25. Richard Wike, Laura Silver and Alexandra Castillo, 'Many Across the Globe Are Dissatisfied with How Democracy Is Working', Pew Research Center, Washington, DC, 29 April 2019; Economist Intelligence Unit, 'Democracy Index 2018', London, 2018; 'Democracy for All?', *The V-Dem Annual Democracy Report 2018*, V-Dem, Gothenburg, 2018; Freedom House, 'Freedom in the World 2018', Washington, DC, 2018; and R.S. Foa et al., 'Youth and Satisfaction with Democracy: Reversing the Democratic Disconnect?', Bennett Institute for Public Policy, Cambridge, October 2020.

26. The various survey findings are analysed in Debasish Roy Chowdhury and John Keane, *To Kill A Democracy*.

27. Ruchir Sharma, 'The Billionaire Boom', *Financial Times*, 15–16 May 2021; Thorstein Veblen, *The Vested Interests and the Common Man*, p. 125.

28. Sheldon Wolin, *Democracy Incorporated: Managed Democracy and the Spectre of Inverted Totalitarianism*, Princeton University Press, Princeton and Oxford, 2008, pp. 286–87.

29. Simon Reid-Henry, *Empire of Democracy: The Remaking of the West Since the Cold War, 1971–2017*, Simon & Schuster, New York and London, 2019, part 1.

30. Su Changhe, 'Western Democracy Must Be Demoted from a Universal Idea to a Local Theory' (需将西方民主从普世知识降级为地方理论), *Guangming Daily*, 28 May 2016, http://news.sina.com.cn/c/2013-05-28/092127244512.shtml; Thomas Hon Wing Polin, 'Democracy: A Western Tool for Domination', *Global Times*, 11 February 2018; the remark by Liu Cixin is cited in Jiaying Fan, 'The War of the Worlds', *The New Yorker*, 24 June 2019, p. 34; the internment is described in Liu Cixin, 'Post-Deterrence Era, Year 2 Australia', *Death's End*, Tor, New York, 2016.

31. John Keane, *The New Despotism*, Harvard University Press, Cambridge and London, 2020.
32. Friedrich Nietzsche, *Twilight of the Idols* (trans. M. Hollingdale), London 1990, pp. ix, 38.
33. Nahum Capen, *The History of Democracy: or, Political Progress, Historically Illustrated, From the Earliest to the Latest Periods*, American Publishing Company, Hartford, 1874, p. v: 'The History of Democracy is a history of principles, as connected with the nature of man and society. All principles centre in God . . . In the sublime truths of Christianity is to be found the high standard of human conduct and endeavour.'
34. James Mill, 'Government' (1820), reprinted as *An Essay on Government*, Cambridge University Press, Cambridge, 1937.
35. Richard Rorty, 'The Priority of Democracy to Philosophy', in Richard Rorty, *Volume I: Objectivity, Relativism, and Truth*, Philosophical Papers, Cambridge University Press, 1991, pp. 257–82; compare my reply to this way of thinking in *The Life and Death of Democracy*, especially pp. 839–72.
36. Barack Obama, address to Rutgers University's 250th anniversary commencement ceremony, 15 May 2016.
37. Jean-Luc Nancy, *The Truth of Democracy*, Fordham University Press, New York, 2010, p. 27.
38. John Keane, 'Silence, Early Warnings and Catastrophes', in *Power and Humility*, pp. 207–22
38. Daniel Kahneman, *Thinking, Fast and Slow*, Penguin Books, London and New York, 2011, p. 418.

Image Credits

p. vi: Dreros law, photograph courtesy of the author; William Blake after Peter Paul Rubens, 'Democritus', 1789, public domain; Nicene Creed, FLHC 39 / Alamy

p. vii: René Louis de Voyer, Alamy; secret ballot, lp studio / Shutterstock; carnation, Oksana2010 / Shutterstock; equality knuckles, Khabarushka / Shutterstock

p. 5: Amanda Phingbodhipakkiya for MoveOn, 2020

p. 9: Keystone Press / Alamy

p. 11: Al'aa Salah, Sudan, April 2019, AFP via Getty Images

p. 12: Cesare Ripa, *Iconologie*, trans. Jean Baudoin, Aux amateurs de livres, Paris, 1643

p. 23: Unknown author via Oriential Institute Museum, Chicago

p. 25: Unknown author via mesopotamiangods.com

p. 27: 'Advice to a Prince', Neo-Assyrian, c. 650BC, excavated by George Smith, Kouyunjik, Iraq. © The Trustees of the British Museum

p. 32: Pushkin State Museum of Fine Arts, Moscow via Wikimedia Commons

p. 34: Photograph courtesy of the author

p. 39: Leo Von Klenze, 'Ideal view of the Acropolis and Areopagus in Athens', 1846, © bpk image agency

p. 43: Ephorate of Antiquities of Athens City, Ancient Agora, ASCSA: Agora Excavations. © Hellenic Ministry of Culture and Sports/Hellenic Organization of Cultural Resources Development. Photographer: Craig Mauzy

p. 46: Rudolf Muller, 'View of the Acropolis from the Pnyx', 1863. © Benaki Museum, Athens

p. 48: Stephan Vanfleteren

p. 51: Ephorate of Antiquities of Athens City, Ancient Agora, ASCSA: Agora

Excavations. © Hellenic Ministry of Culture and Sports/Hellenic Organization of Cultural Resources Development

p. 54: Ephorate of Antiquities of Athens City, Ancient Agora, ASCSA: Agora Excavations. © Hellenic Ministry of Culture and Sports/Hellenic Organization of Cultural Resources Development

p. 56: Pictorial Press Ltd / Alamy

p. 58: Unknown author

p. 61: Philip von Foltz, 'The Funeral Oration of Pericles', 1852. The Picture Art Collection / Alamy

p. 74: Glenn O Coleman, 'Election Night Bonfire', 1928, Detroit Institute of Arts, USA © Detroit Institute of Arts/Founders Society, Purchase, Mrs. James Couzens, via Bridgeman Images

p. 76: Historical Images Archive/Alamy

p. 81: John Keyse Sherwin after William Hogarth, 'The Politician', 1775, De Luan/Alamy

p. 88: Miguel Hermoso Cuesta via Wikimedia Commons

p. 90: Rosegarten Museum via Wikimedia Commons

p. 95: Unknown author via Wikimedia Commons

p. 99: Unknown author, first published in *The Daily Mail*, United Kingdom, 1909

p. 101: Aristotle, *Politica: Le livre de politiques*, translated by Nicholas Oresme, 14th century, Royal Library of Belgium

p. 102: James Gillray, 'Charles James Fox, "A democrat; - or - reason and philosophy"', published by Hannah Humphrey, 1793, © National Portrait Gallery, London

p. 110: William Rider-Rider, 1917, Canada. Dept. of National Defence, Library and Archives Canada

p. 116: José Clemente Orozco, 'Las Masas (The Masses)', 1935 via Alamy

p. 124: Unknown author via Wikimedia Commons

p. 129: Foto News / Archivio Luce

p. 136: Unknown author via *Asahi Shimbun*

p. 145: Gideon Mendel/Getty Images

p. 148: Associated Press

p. 150: Unknown author via Kingsandqueensofportgual.tumblr

p. 153: Sueddeutsche Zeitung Photo/Alamy

Image Credits

p. 157: Godong/Alamy

p. 160: Unknown author

p. 174: © United Nations Photo

p. 179: Photo – Thomas Dorrington, courtesy of Extinction Rebellion Cambridge

p. 186: ITAR-TASS News Agency/Alamy

p. 191: Unknown author

Index

Index